VINTAGE
CASE TRACTORS

Peter Letourneau

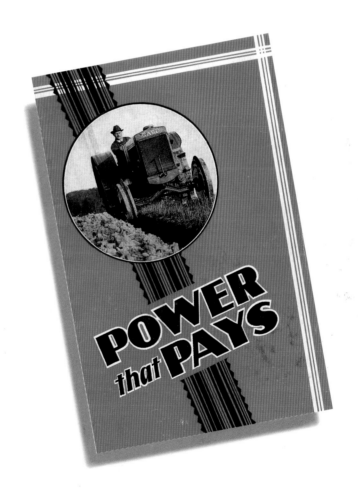

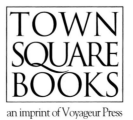

an imprint of Voyageur Press

Edited by Michael Dregni
Designed by Andrea Rud
Printed in Hong Kong

97 98 99 00 01   5   4   3   2   1

Library of Congress Cataloging-in-Publication Data
Letourneau, Peter A., 1950–
    Vintage case tractors / by Peter Letourneau.
        p.   cm.
    Includes bibliographical references and index.
    ISBN 0-89658-335-X
    1. Case tractors—History. I. Title.
TL233.6.C37L48   1997
629.225—dc20   96-35225
                                  CIP

A Town Square Book
Published by Voyageur Press, Inc.
123 North Second Street, P.O. Box 338, Stillwater, MN 55082 U.S.A.
612-430-2210, fax 612-430-2211

Distributed in Canada by Raincoast Books
8680 Cambie Street, Vancouver, B.C. V6P 6M9

Distributed in Europe by Midland Publishing Ltd.
24 The Hollow, Earl Shilton, Leicester LE9 7NA, England
Tel: 01455 233747

Page 1: 1918 Case Model 20/40 Gasoline Tractor.

Page 1, inset: Model 12/25 Ad, circa 1910s
Case promoted the dependability of its Model 12/25 gas-and-oil tractor since this was a major concern of farmers who were considering making the move from steam-powered to gas-powered machines.

Page 2–3: Case 110-hp Steamer
Before the days of the big, high-powered steam tractors, the prairie sod of the Midwest was all but impenetrable to farmers working with horse- or oxen-pulled plows. The centuries-old turf was made up of buffalo grass and other native species growing out of the rich, heavy soil. Case's heavy-duty 110-hp steamer was the ideal machine to break the prairie sod and allow modern agriculture to expand westward. This Case 110-hp steamer was pictured at the 1989 Rollag, Minnesota, threshing show. It is owned by Jim Briden of Fargo, North Dakota, and Norman Pross of Luvern, North Dakota. (Photograph © by Dave Arnold)

Page 3, inset: Case Catalog, circa 1930s

Page 5, top: 1913 Case Model 12/25 Gasoline Tractor.

Page 5, bottom: Replacing the Horse
In brochures such as this, Case promoted the savings gained by farming with tractors. Citing farmers who disposed of their horses after buying a Case Crossmotor, the brochure states Case tractors "are rapidly replacing the old, unreliable and less efficient animal power, thereby increasing the farmers' profit by lowering the cost of production."

Contents

Chapter 1

In the Beginning

The Visionary J. I. Case

At the heart of successful threshing Case Machinery is always to be found.
—J. I. Case Threshing Machine Company
catalog, 1900s

LEFT: Jerome Increase Case's Vision
J. I. Case had a vision of the mechanized farm using Case machinery from plowing to threshing. Still going strong in 1948, this 1915 Case Model 65 steam traction engine powers a 1912 Case 32x54-inch (80x135-cm) steel threshing machine. Its rigid platform frame construction, substantial draw bar, and ideal gearing ensured heavy-duty work performance.

ABOVE: Case Eagle Trademark
Case adopted the now-famous eagle trademark in 1865. It was patterned after "Old Abe," a magnificent bald eagle that had served in the Civil War as the mascot for the 8th Wisconsin Regiment, Company C, and was named after President Abraham Lincoln. In 1894, the Eagle trademark adopted this present form, perched on top of the world.

Ground-Hog Thresher, circa 1842
Young Jerome Increase Case first learned about the ground-hog thresher in the Genesee Farmer *magazine. A marvel of its time, the machine threshed from 150 to 200 bushels of wheat per day when operated by horse tread power. Jerome convinced his father, Caleb, to become the local agent in New York state for the ground-hog manufacturer. Jerome soon mastered the device and traveled about in New York's Oswego County doing custom threshing, and demonstrating to area farmers the superiority of the ground-hog. Convinced that the Wisconsin territory was the next great national breadbasket, Case bought six ground-hogs on credit and in 1842, boarded the ship* Vandalia *bound for Chicago. From Chicago he "threshed" his way to Rochester, Wisconsin, selling all but one ground-hog. He spent his irst winter in Wisconsin improving the crude thresher and conceiving his own thresher. This ground-hog thresher is similar to that sold by Jerome Increase Case in 1842.*

"In 1842 Jerome I. Case, an ambitious youth, left his home in New York and landed in Racine, Wisconsin. Soon after his arrival he started a small workshop, it was little more than an ordinary blacksmith shop. He was the only worker. Such was the modest beginning. Years of toil were ahead. Yet this man had an ideal—a practical one—and he stuck to the job year in and year out. From a farmer's family himself, he saw a vision. . . ."

With these words published in a seventy-fifth anniversary album in 1917, the venerable J. I. Case Threshing Machine Company celebrated its threshers, steam and gas tractors, and a full line of farming implements that were sold throughout the world.

Jerome Increase Case, the company's founder, was indeed a visionary. He was one of the great pioneers of North American agriculture alongside such farming luminaries as John Deere, Cyrus Hall McCormick, Henry Ford, and few others. Besides farm machinery, Case also built automobiles and dabbled with airplanes at the dawn of the age of flight. In addition, he served as mayor of Racine and eventually was elected to the Wisconsin Senate. His life was rich in successes, and his legacy is still with us today in the current crop of Case tractors plowing the fields of North America, more than one hundred and fifty years after the firm's founding.

In 1842, twenty-two-year-old J. I. Case set up his blacksmithery in Rochester, Wisconsin; the firm considers this year the founding date of the Case company. In the spring of 1844, Case demonstrated his new creation: Beginning with a simple thresher, he crafted one of the first combined threshing and cleaning machines—a mechanical means to both thresh grain and remove the chaff in one operation. By fall, Case began producing his new machine in a facility he built in Racine. From the beginning, demand for Case's threshers exceeded supply, and his Racine Threshing Machine Works prospered. The company soon became an early leader in the manufacture of mechanical harvesting equipment.

The pioneering threshers were stationary machines driven by horse-power units. The earliest power units were nothing more than inclined treadmills upon which horses or oxen walked in place. As the animals walked and the treadmill advanced, a large pulley was turned, and a belt transferred power to the thresher. Mechanical threshers quickly gained acceptance, and demand for larger-capacity threshers soon followed.

Larger machines required more horsepower. Although treadmills

Case Dingee-Woodbury Sweep Horsepower

THE Case Dingee-Woodbury horsepower is familiar to thousands of old threshermen. It is well known because of its power and lightness of draft. Side strains are prevented by double bull pinions. Shaft is held in perfect alinement by spur wheel-shaft which is supported by adjustable babbitted box. It has metal frame, steel truck wheels with four-inch tires. Equalizer sheaves fit perfectly, preventing undue wear. The sweeps of the 12-horsepower are 12 feet 7 inches long and 14 feet long for the 14-horsepower size. The use of a 16-tooth cog pinion, which gives 101 revolutions of the tumbling rod to one round of horses, will in most cases give proper cylinder speed to a Case threshing machine.

were built that could accommodate more than one horse, there were practical limits to the number of animals that could share a treadmill—two or perhaps three at a time. A more efficient and effective means of generating and transferring power was created with the mechanical sweep.

A mechanical power sweep or "horsepower" was a device to which a number of horses or oxen were tethered. With the simplest such devices, the animals walked in a circle around the power sweep, turning a central vertical shaft as they advanced. Gears then transferred power from the rotating vertical shaft to a horizontal shaft. The rotating horizontal shaft, over which the horses stepped as they circled the unit, was coupled to the thresher's gear-driven mechanism. Power sweeps could harness the energy of as many as eighteen horses, and provided significantly more power than was available from treadmills. In combination with a power sweep, threshers of the early 1860s could process three hundred to four hundred bushels per day. Due to advances in thresher technology, output more than doubled by the end of the decade.

While such increases in productivity were impressive, the best was yet to come. By the late 1840s, portable steam power had emerged on American farms. A number of companies offered steam engines mounted on heavy wooden chassis. Pulled by horse or oxen, portable steam engines were expensive, cumbersome, and complicated to operate and maintain. Still, portable steam power revolutionized agriculture. Steam engines operated at a uniform pace and were a nearly unlimited source of power. Unlike animals that required constant care, feed, rest, and shelter, steam engines could work continuously and under the most hostile conditions. They required virtually no attention when not in use, were easily stored in a limited space, yet were quickly available when needed.

Case Dingee-Woodbury Sweep Horsepower, 1917
Case's mechanical power sweep, the Case Dingee-Woodbury Sweep Horsepower. The unit was sold in twelve- and fourteen-horse models. Case hired Dingee-Woodbury's designer and purchased the manufacturing rights to the horsepower in 1878. Forty years later, the horsepower was still offered in the company's machinery catalog, a testament to the power's proven ability—as well as to the longevity of horse farming.

ABOVE: Case Separator Threshing Machine

J. I. Case began as a thresherman. Before the Case company made its name building steam-powered tractors, the firm made a line of pioneering and innovative separator threshing machines. By the 1850s, Case was the name in threshers. The early threshers were built of wood, but in 1904, Case created its breakthrough all-metal thresher. This Case separator was displayed at the famous Rollag, Minnesota, threshing show. (Photograph © by Dave Arnold)

RIGHT: Case Logo

This beautiful and intricate Case logo graces the side of one of the firm's famous all-metal threshers. (Photograph © by Dave Arnold)

Jerome Increase Case, Man of Vision

The J. I. Case Threshing Machine Company has always been justly proud of its heritage and long history of building thoroughbred farm equipment. In the firm's annual catalogs, the corporate history was promoted as proof of the company's long-standing commitment to quality and honesty. This excerpt from a World War I–era Case Power Farming Machinery catalog was typical of the sales pitch of the day:

The J. I. Case Threshing Machine Company was founded in 1842, over three-quarters of a century ago, by Jerome I. Case. The beginning of this institution was the outcome of a vision—an ideal, if such we may call it. Mr. Case was determined to give the farmers a better threshing machine than there was on the market. He started in a small workshop; it was little more than a blacksmith shop. With years of toil ahead, but with grim determination, he soon succeeded. Each year brought increased business. He believed in honest value—he believed in fair dealing. On this code of business principles which he then established, his business grew gradually and constantly. Farmer passed the word to farmer and soon the Case name became universally famous. Today the Case line includes threshers, tractors, balers, silo fillers, road machinery, in fact a complete line of power farming equipment.

In all these years we have followed the principles laid down by Jerome I. Case, the founder. We know that to build right and to deal right always pays. Honesty is the only and best policy. In the line of Case power farming machinery described in this booklet is represented quality. We believe and thousands of farmers know that when they get Case machinery their dollar is invested wisely and safely. Buying a Case product means satisfaction guaranteed. It is on a complete satisfaction basis that we ask you to consider Case machinery for your farm.

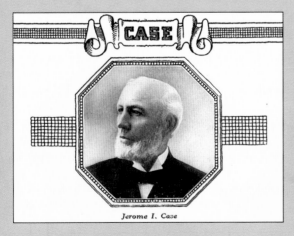

Jerome Increase Case

The great and increasing demand for my Threshing Machines has induced me to enlarge my establishment, attach an Iron Furnace, and put in Steam Power. For the last four years I have not been able to supply more than one-half the orders I have received for Machines; but I have now the largest and most commodious shops west of Buffalo, and hope, in the future, to be able to supply all who may wish a superb Threshing Machine.
—Racine Threshing Machine Works announcement, 1856

Vintage Case Tractors Timeline

This timeline of Case events comes from "A Case History" brochure distributed by Case in the early 1970s. Events since the 1970s have been added to the timeline.

1842: Jerome Increase Case (1819–1891) founded the J. I. Case Threshing Machine Company in Rochester, Wisconsin, by improving a crude "ground-hog" thresher that he had brought with him when he emigrated from Williamstown, New York.

1844: Jerome Case moved to Racine, Wisconsin, when the citizens of Rochester refused to give him water-power rights for his planned factory. In Racine, he started to manufacture crude threshers, improving them as new models were built.

1847: Case erected a three-story shop in Racine that became the hub of his farm equipment manufacturing business.

1848: The company became the leading industrial employer and the largest employer in Racine.

1852: J. I. Case was busy demonstrating his thresher to farmers across the Midwest, apparently with much success.

1862: A much-improved sweep power, the Mounted Woodbury, was added. The "Sweepstakes" thresher, first of Case's "name" threshers, could thresh 200–300 bushels per day.

1863: J. I. Case took in three partners to form J. I. Case and Company. The men who soon became known as "The Big Four" included Massena Erskine, Robert Baker, and Stephen Bull.

1865: The now-famous Eagle trademark was adopted.

1865: The "Eclipse" thresher was introduced to "eclipse" all others of the day.

1869: The first Case steam engine was produced—to be followed by 36,000 more over the years. Old Number 1 was on wheels, but it was drawn by horses and used only for belt power.

1876: A steam traction engine was developed, and it was awarded a gold medal for excellence at the Centennial Exposition in Philadelphia. Five hundred Case steam engines were now in use on American farms, and seventy-five were sold during this year.

1877: Steam engine sales increased to 109 during this year.

1878: Steam engine sales doubled over the previous year to 220. The Company shipped its first thresher overseas.

1880: J. I. Case Threshing Machine Company was incorporated.

1880: The "Agitator" thresher was developed and proved popular because of increased efficiency and capacity.

1884: J. I. Case became involved in an incident that has come to typify the company's continuing determination to build high-quality products. A Case thresher on a Minnesota farm would not perform up to par. Despite efforts of the dealer and then a plant mechanic, the machine refused to function properly. Finally, J. I. Case himself traveled the distance to fix the machine that bore his name. Before a large crowd, amazed that the president of the company would travel all that way, J. I. Case worked on his thresher. It still wouldn't work. Disgusted that such a product had left his factory, he doused it with kerosene and set it ablaze. The next day the farmer was presented with a new, perfectly operating Case thresher.

1886: A steering device was added to the steam traction engine, thereby dispensing with the need for horses. At this time, Case was the largest manufacturer of steam engines in the world.

1891: J. I. Case died and Stephen Bull, his brother-in-law, became president.

1892: The Company developed its first gasoline tractor—in appearance it was much like a steam engine. It was commercially unsuccessful due to lack of proper ignition and carburetion equipment.

1894: The Case Eagle trademark adopted its famous trademark form, perched on top of the world.

1899: Around the turn of the century a distributor was appointed in Odessa, Russia.

1900: A distributorship agreement was signed with an Australian firm in Melbourne.

1901: Frank K. Bull, son of Stephen Bull, became president of Case. The company was now shipping its threshing machines via special trains. These consisted of oversize red, white, and blue flatcars carrying the threshers to market while accompanied by a calliope.

1904: Case brought out the first all-steel thresher. Although ridiculed by many, it was soon copied by all other manufacturers.

1910: The small Pierce Motor Company of Racine (no connection with Pierce-Arrow) was purchased and Case started building high-quality automobiles in the luxury class.

1911: The Model 30/60 gas traction engine took the gold medal in the Winnipeg Plowing Contest.

1911: Three Case racing cars were entered in the first Indianapolis 500 race, occupying the pole position and two spots in the second row.

1913: The Case Tractor Works, south of Racine and now known as the Clausen Works, was built for the manufacture of several sizes of four-cylinder gas tractors, several models having cross-mounted engines.

1919: Case purchased the Grand Detour Plow Company in Grand Detour, Illinois, to add a line of plows and some tillage tools. This was the first step toward becoming a full-line farm machinery manufacturer.

1923: The 100,000th thresher came off the assembly line. In this same year production of large grain combines began, rapidly making the thresher obsolete in the Great Plains area. Nevertheless, Case continued to build threshers for another thirty years as farmers were slow to accept the "new-fangled" combines.

1924: Production of automobiles and steam engines was discontinued.

1928: The company name was changed to the J. I. Case Company. The Emerson-Brantingham line of tillage, haying, and harvesting equipment built at Rockford, Illinois, was purchased.

1929: The Model L tractor with unit-type frame construction was introduced, followed by Models C and CC.

1932: The company introduced a one-man combine with power take-off drive, and a successful two-row corn picker.

1937: Case purchased the Rock Island Plow Company factory in Illinois, and a factory at Burlington, Iowa, for the manufacture of small combines.

1939: Flambeau Red became the identifying color for Case equipment with the introduction of a new fleet of tractors, including the D Series.

1940: The S and V Series of tractors were introduced. The Eagle hitch and hydraulic controls were added later.

1941: The Company became engaged in wartime military manufacturing.

1942: Case celebrated its centennial year with a pageant at Union Grove, Wisconsin. An historical display was entered in the annual July 4th parade.

1953: Case put the Model 500 diesel tractor on the market and it was acclaimed the finest diesel available.

1955: The Company introduced the 400 Series tractors in gasoline, diesel, and LP-gas models.

1956: Case introduced the 300 Series tractors primarily for smaller-sized farms.

1957: The American Tractor Corporation, manufacturer of crawler tractors and earth-moving equipment at Churubusco, Indiana, was merged with Case.

1964: The highlight of 1964 was the acquisition of controlling interest in the company by Kern County Land Company of San Francisco. This resulted in a refinancing plan that built a solid foundation for Case's future operations.

1965: Old Abe celebrated his 100th anniversary as the company trademark.

1967: Reorganization of the company establishing separate agricultural and construction equipment divisions. Kern County Land Company (majority stockholder of Case) joins with Tenneco Inc., Houston, Texas, world's largest distributor of natural gas.

1984: Tenneco buys International Harvester after the giant of the agricultural industry suffered massive losses due to the 1980s farm crisis.

1988: Tenneco restructures and Case-IH becomes its largest division.

1994: Tenneco spun off the Case Corporation as a new company with tractors and other farming and construction products labeled as Case-IH machines.

Chapter 2

When Steam Was King

Development of the Case Steamers, 1876–1924

*A good steam engineer should be sober, industrious, careful,
and faithful to his charge.*
—Case's *Young Engineer's Guide* steam-engine instruction book

LEFT: *This 110-hp Case steamer is owned by Kevin Anderson and David Fie and is
based in Andover, South Dakota.* (Photograph © by Dave Arnold)

ABOVE: Case Steamer Catalog, 1916

Today Case machinery is used throughout the world. Under every flag are farmers who know and respect the Case emblem. This record has been built on Quality Products. That which is best is destined to endure.
—Case brochure, 1910s

Steam power revolutionized farming. When coupled to steam power, thresher output was greatly enhanced. By 1870, Case claimed that its steam-driven Eclipse thresher could separate up to two thousand bushels a day. With such impressive results, it is easy to understand why Case began to build steam engines.

The first Case steam engine was built in 1876. It was a 10-horsepower portable—but not self-propelled—unit. Case soon built a smaller 8-hp unit as well, and within three years sold more than five hundred steam engines.

Portable steam power was made even more practicable with the arrival of gearing and, later, steering mechanisms that transformed portable engines into self-propelled "traction" engines. Case built its first chain-drive traction engine in 1878 and its first self-steering machine in 1884.

By 1884, Case offered steam engines as skid, portable, and tractive units in a range from 8 to 30 hp. In 1887, Case built its first gear-drive traction model; within a decade it offered steam traction units with friction-type clutches. By 1900, most Case steam traction engines featured spring-mounted engines, which reduced strain on the boilers as the tractors traveled over rough terrain. Such improvements to steam traction units made large-scale plowing with steam possible, and by 1902, a 25-hp Case steamer could pull ten 16-inch (40-cm) plow bottoms.

Case built steam engines as small as 6 hp and as large as 150 hp. At one time or another, Case built direct-flue and return-flue steam engines, in both simple and compound configurations, and both center-crank and side-crank engines. Engines were built to burn either coal, wood, straw, fuel oil, or a combination of fuels.

Although gasoline tractors were introduced around 1902, they did not displace steam overnight. The U.S. Department of Agriculture reported in 1933 that the use of steam power peaked in 1910 when some 72,000 steam engines were employed on American farms. Of the more than 175 American and Canadian companies manufacturing portable or traction steam engines in the years between 1850 and 1930, Case led them all in sales. Case steam engine sales reached a zenith in 1912, but by 1915, Case was building more gasoline than steam units. Case terminated production of steam engines in 1924, after building nearly 36,000 steam engines.

The days when steam was king had come to a close.

ABOVE: Case 110-hp Steamer
Production records indicate that the first 110-hp tractor was built in 1910 and the last in 1913. However, the tractor was still prominently featured in the 1917 and 1918 sales catalogs. (Photograph © by Dave Arnold)

RIGHT: Case Steamer, 1907
Steam traction engines were sold for construction use as well as farm work. In this photo from 1907, a Case steam engine provided the power necessary to pull construction equipment used to repair and grade roads and streets in the Racine, Wisconsin, area. The contractor pictured here, James Cape & Sons, Co., is still in business today and uses an extensive variety of Case construction and utility equipment in its work.

FACING PAGE, BOTTOM: Case Steamer Line, 1916
J. I. Case Threshing Machine Company's 1916 lineup of steam engines included engines in eight sizes: 30, 40, 50, 60, 65, 75, 80, and a mammoth 110 hp.

Not to do away with the horse, but to take the heavy burdens from his shoulder—that is the tractor farming idea. Every man who loves horses has often wished that the killing work of plowing and disking and harvesting might be done in some other way. Now many farmers are doing it in another way, horses are kept in better condition and better spirits, and feed bills are reduced.
—Prairie Farmer, 1915

g Machine Cor. Center & 13th Sts. Marshall Photo ...

19

Case 30-hp Steamer, 1917

In 1917, Case again offered eight traction engines ranging in size from 30 to 110 hp. The four-plow, 30-hp model engine was a single-cylinder, or "simple," example of 7½x10-inch (187.5x250-mm) bore and stroke. The 40-hp tractor was a simple cylinder of 8¼x10 inches (206x250 mm) and developed 63.35 brake hp at 267.5 rpm during the 1913 Winnipeg trials. The 50-hp tractor was a simple cylinder of 9x10 inches (225x250 mm). The 60-hp tractor was a simple cylinder of 10x10 inches (250x250 mm). The 65-hp tractor, with simple cylinder of 10x11 inches (250x275 mm), was a popular model from 1914 through 1924. The 75- and 80-hp models both featured a simple-cylinder engine of 11x11 inches (275x275 mm). The models varied in boiler steam pressures and the number and lengths of boiler tubes, as well as in overall tractor dimensions. The 80-hp developed 109.9 brake hp during the 1913 Winnipeg trials. Canopies, headlights, and extension rims were among attachments offered on all models.

Pressure Gauge

The all-important pressure gauge on a Case steamer. (Photograph © by Dave Arnold)

In the Last Days of the Steam Engine

By the late 1910s, the writing was on the wall: The newfangled gasoline and kerosene tractors were the way of the future. But Case had built its reputation on its gigantic steam engines, and it continued to produce, promote, and sell its steamers in the dawning days of the gas tractor's supremacy. This excerpt from the firm's catalog shows the unflinching dedication Case felt for its steamers—even while the firm was marketing its first gas tractors:

With the advent of kerosene and gasoline tractors, many manufacturers immediately switched their interest from steam engines to the newer field. But not so with Case.

For Case has become the leader in the steam engine world—a position which we are not likely to endanger. So instead of diminishing our interest in the steam engine division, we increased it. We figured that from a strategic standpoint this is the time to forever insure Case leadership.

While our tractor department has made remarkable gains in the past few years—astounding gains—we know that in some localities steam has always been and always will be the most satisfactory power. Time will prove.

So we have gone on with even greater ambition, adding new refinements and features to our steam engine line. Wherever new ideas have presented themselves, our engineers and experts have tested out all of them. We have discarded certain ideas—added others. We choose only the best.

Today, we know that Case steam engines represent the pinnacle in quality, simplicity, efficiency, performance, durability, and economy.

We know that in Case steam engines results may be had that cannot be obtained elsewhere. We know that no other steam engine has the tradition behind it, the years of experience and experiment, and the many friends. And we feel all of these things are known by thousands, yes, hundreds of thousands of progressive farmers and threshermen.

Our line of steam tractors is complete—eight sizes. In our great million-and-a-half-dollar steam engine shops we have a capacity of ten machines per day. Here are built Case steam engines complete, from the raw material to the finished product. Here master foundrymen, machinists, and workmen use material approved by our laboratories, and bought in large quantities by an exacting purchasing department.

We save for the American farmers millions of dollars each year, and at the same time bring values into Case steam engines which could not be possible in a smaller organization, less experienced.

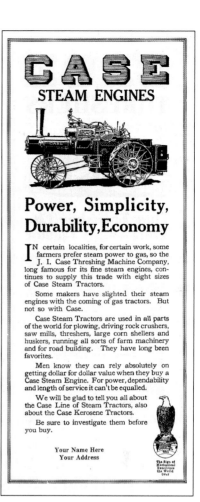

Case Steamer Ad, 1918
Case continued to build steam tractors for more than a decade following the introduction of gas tractors. In this ad from 1918, Case stated, "Some makers have slighted their steam engines with the coming of gas tractors. But not so with Case."

With the advent of kerosene and gasoline tractors, many manufacturers immediately switched their interest from steam engines to the newer field. But not so with Case. For Case has become the leader in the steam engine world—a position which we are not likely to endanger. So instead of diminishing our interest in the steam engine division, we increased it.
—Case brochure, 1910s

ABOVE: Case 110-hp Steamer
From the front end, the smoke box and smokestack of this steamer are clearly visible. Mounted above the feed water heater is the governor. (Photograph © by Dave Arnold)

RIGHT, TOP: Case 110-hp Steamer
Fully loaded and ready for work, a 110-hp tractor weighs about 35,000 pounds (15,750 kg). (Photograph © by Dave Arnold)

RIGHT, BOTTOM: Case Steamers at Work
A duo of steamers break the prairie sod at the 1989 Rollag, Minnesota, threshing show. Following the lead tractor is a Case 110-hp steamer. (Photograph © by Dave Arnold)

ABOVE: Case Power Steering Mechanism
This Case 110-hp steamer featured mechanically assisted power steering. (Photograph © by Dave Arnold)

LEFT, TOP: Case Steamer Rear Wheel
The rear wheel on this Case 110-hp steamer is about as tall as the operator. (Photograph © by Dave Arnold)

LEFT, BOTTOM: Transmission Gearing, 1917
Case moved from chain drive to gear traction in the late 1880s. In this model from 1917, as with all Case steam tractors of this period, both rear wheels were powered. This view shows the differential and transmission gearing. Open gearing, exposed to dirt and mud, was the norm in this period.

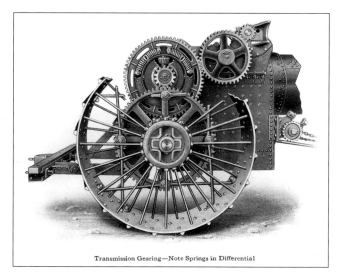

Transmission Gearing—Note Springs in Differential

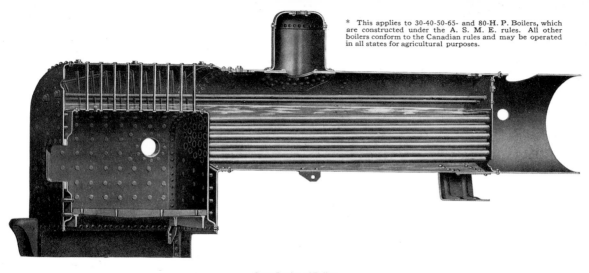

Cross Section of Boiler

FACING PAGE, TOP: Case Direct-Flue Boiler, 1917
Cutaway view of a Case direct-flue boiler. Smoke and heat passed from the firebox at the rear, through the flues and out the stack (not pictured) at the opposite end. Water circulated around the flues and was heated to the boiling point.

BELOW, LEFT: Boiler Cutaway
A cutaway display boiler shows how the steamers worked. The fire box, in the lower left section, heated the boiler, which filled the long, horizontal section with smoke tubes running horizontally through the boiler. The smoke box was situated at the front with the smokestack on top. (Photograph © by Dave Arnold)

BELOW, RIGHT: Case Steamer Details, 1917
The boiler was the most critical component of a Case steam engine. Case advertised that the "actual strength of all parts of the boiler must be at least five times as great as allowable working pressure." By 1900, Case boilers were mounted on springs to cushion shock during movement.

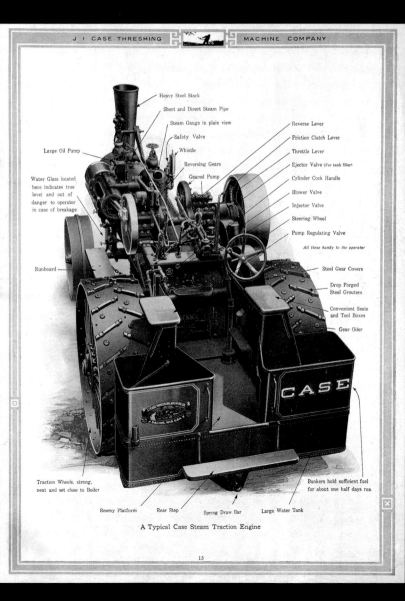

J I CASE THRESHING MACHINE COMPANY

Heavy Steel Stack

Short and Direct Steam Pipe

Steam Gauge in plain view

Reverse Lever

Friction Clutch Lever

Safety Valve

Throttle Lever

Large Oil Pump

Whistle

Ejector Valve (For tank filler)

Reversing Gears

Cylinder Cock Handle

Geared Pump

Blower Valve

Water Glass located here indicates true level and out of danger to operator in case of breakage

Injector Valve

Steering Wheel

Pump Regulating Valve

All these handy to the operator

Runboard

Steel Gear Covers

Drop Forged Steel Grouters

Convenient Seats and Tool Boxes

Gear Oiler

CASE

Traction Wheels, strong, neat and set close to Boiler

Bunkers hold sufficient fuel for about one half days run

Roomy Platform   Rear Step   Spring Draw Bar   Large Water Tank

A Typical Case Steam Traction Engine

15

The Case organization feels that with farmers it has a great mission in serving the peoples of the world. This has been our life work.
—Case brochure, 1910s

RIGHT: Case 110-hp Steamer
This 110-hp Case steamer is owned by Kevin Anderson and David Fie and based in Andover, South Dakota. This steamer was made from a collection of parts from many similar units as well as specially made parts that the restorers could not locate. (Photograph © by Dave Arnold)

BELOW: Case 110-hp Steamer
The 110-hp steamer was able to pull ten 14-inch (35-cm) plow bottoms. (Photograph © by Dave Arnold)

Case 150-hp Boiler
(Photograph © by Dave Arnold)

Case 110-hp Steamer
The 110-hp steamer developed a whopping 144.22 brake hp at the 1913 Winnipeg trials. (Photograph © by Dave Arnold)

Case Steam Roller
Case also built 10- and 12-ton (9,000- and 10,800-kg) heavy-duty steam road rollers for road construction. The 10-ton model was introduced in 1910, and was based on the 65-hp simple-cylinder engine. This steam roller was on display at the 1994 Rollag show. (Photograph © by Dave Arnold)

27

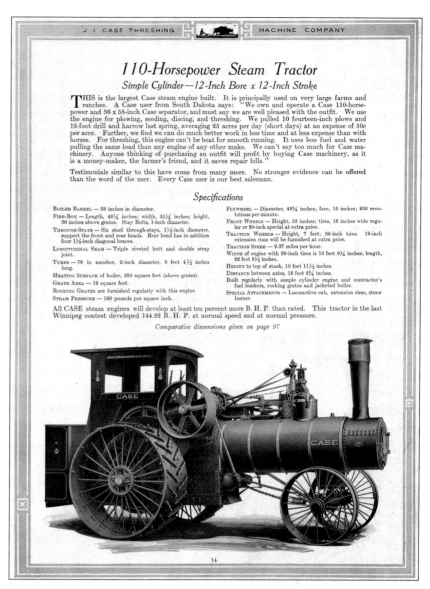

ABOVE: Case 110-hp Steamer, 1917
Although Case did build a few 14x14-inch (350x350-mm), 150-hp "road locomotives," the Case 110-hp, with 12x12-inch (300x300-mm) simple-cylinder engine, was the largest and most legendary Case steam tractor.

LEFT, TOP: Case 110-hp Steamer
One of the few remaining Case 110-hp steamers, on display at the 1989 Rollag, Minnesota, threshing show. (Photograph © by Dave Arnold)

FACING PAGE, INSET: Feed Water Heater
The green-painted cylinder contains a series of smaller pipes through which feed water is directed. This feed water heater uses spent steam on its way to the smokestack to preheat the water being fed to the boiler. This heater is on a 110-hp Case steamer. (Photograph © by Dave Arnold)

Chapter 3

Dawn of the Gasoline Tractor

Pioneering Work with the Gas-Engined Tractor, 1894–1916

Some light duty tractors we know are so designed as to operate up to four miles an hour. This policy we believe is wrong, as it is most extravagant and is unproductive of the best results.
—Case catalog, 1918

LEFT: Model 20/40
A Case Model 20/40 gasoline tractor on display at the 1989 Western Minnesota Steam Threshers Reunion held in Rollag, Minnesota. (Photograph © by Dave Arnold)

ABOVE: Lineup of Old and New Models, circa 1910s
This catalog displayed Case's line of old- and new-generation models, all hitched to the firm's Grand Detour plows. The 12/25 and 20/40 were of the older gas-and-oil generation, whereas the 9/18 and 10/20 signaled the dawn of the Crossmotor era.

Paterson's Balanced Gas Engine, circa 1892

Engineer William Paterson of Stockton, California, came to Case in Racine to build an experimental gas engine in the early 1890s. The "balanced" engine was a horizontal two-cylinder inline with water-jacketed combustion chambers. The Paterson was one of the first practical gasoline tractors, and it worked—but not well enough for it to enter production. The Paterson suffered from ignition and carburetion problems, the bane of all early gasoline engines. Undeterred, Paterson patented his engine design on October 30, 1894.

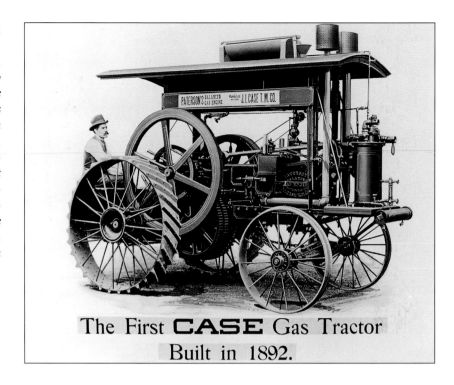

The First CASE Gas Tractor Built in 1892.

The infant gas tractor can stand the emergency endurance test where the horse and the mule fall down. He will pull all your tillage apparatus by moonlight as well as by daylight. If there is no moon all you have to do is to attach a searchlight.
—Barton W. Currie,
The Tractor, 1916

Nicolaus August Otto patented the four-cycle gasoline-powered internal-combustion engine in Germany in 1876. Although crude, Otto's engine was revolutionary. But when Otto's patent rights were invalidated in 1890, hundreds of manufacturers around the world quickly entered into the production of gasoline engines.

Long heralded as the king of steam, J. I. Case Threshing Machine Company nevertheless took early note of the internal-combustion engine and built one of the first gasoline tractors. Case hired inventors William and James Paterson of Stockton, California, to build an experimental gasoline tractor. The novel machine was patented in 1894 and was powered by the Paterson's Balanced Gas Engine, a two-cylinder, four-cycle engine. The chassis and drivetrain were constructed largely of parts similar to those used on Case steam tractors.

In a 1942 interview, David Pryce Davies, a Case vice-president who worked with the Patersons, related that the Paterson tractor featured "one forward speed only . . . reverse being accomplished by sliding a key which could be shifted into neutral position or into forward or reverse speeds. One of the gears driven by the key was operated direct from the pinion on the crankshaft, and the other by means of an idler interposed between it and the pinion to the crankshaft."

As with other early gas tractors, the Paterson tractor suffered from problems with poor carburetion and ignition. Consequently, power output was insufficient for practicable use. William Paterson oversaw the building of a second tractor with an engine of increased displacement; however, it too was hampered by its carburetion and ignition.

Case management soon concluded there was little reason to continue its pioneering experiments with gasoline tractors. Although work stopped and the Paterson tractors were eventually scrapped, Case did not entirely abandon the gasoline engine. During the years from 1895 to 1898, the firm built hundreds of stationary gasoline engines known as the Raymond Improved Gas Engine under license from J. W. Raymond of Chicago.

Revival of the Case Gas Tractor: Model 30/60 of 1912–1916

By 1910, Case committed itself once again to production of a gasoline tractor, and at least one prototype of the Model 60 was built that fall. In January 1912, Case signed a contract with Minneapolis Steel & Machinery Company of Minneapolis, Minnesota, manufacturer of the Twin City tractor, to build five hundred of Case's 60-hp gas tractors. Although not all five hundred were built, the Model 60 (known after 1915 as the Model 30/60) established Case as a contender in the budding gasoline tractor industry.

The Model 30/60 resembled Case's steam tractor in appearance. It was a heavyweight machine weighing close to thirteen tons (11,700 kg) carried on a massive chassis featuring 42-inch (105-cm) front wheels and 72-inch (180-cm) rear wheels. The engine was a transverse-mounted, horizontal two-cylinder of 10x12-inch (250x300-mm) bore and stroke. It was rated at 30 hp at the drawbar and 60 hp at the belt; this is why it subsequently became known in the industry as a 30/60 tractor. The transmission featured two forward speeds and reverse. The drive gears were exposed to the elements, as with most tractors of the day.

The 30/60 was started on gasoline, then the operator switched to a lower-grade fuel. The engine was fitted with a low-tension "make-and-break" ignition and oscillating magneto. Lubrication was by mechanical oiler. Cooling was by induced draft whereby hot exhaust gasses passed from the engine to the top of a cooling tank inside which a tubular-type radiator was fitted. The draft created as the hot gasses escaped from the tank pulled air through the radiator and cooled the water. A pump circulated the 170 gallons (646 liters) of cooling water through the closed system.

Model 30/60 Prototype, 1911
Development work began in 1910 on what would become the first production Case gasoline tractor, the Model 60, later known as the Model 30/60. Production eventually ran from 1912 through 1916, with 493 units being built.

The Old Reliable Model 20/40 of 1912–1919

Arriving immediately after the 30/60, the Case Model 40, or 20/40, proved to be a winner and Case built more than 4,200 units between 1912 and 1919.

Although it generally resembled the 30/60, the 20/40 engine differed from that of the larger tractor. The engine was initially built by the Davis Motor Company of Milwaukee. It was a two-cylinder horizontal opposed engine of 7¾x8-inch (194x200-mm) bore and stroke.

In 1913, Case began production of its own engine of similar construction. The Case-built motor featured a 8x9-inch (200x225-mm) bore and stroke that was eventually increased to 8¾x9 inches (219x225 mm). Lubrication was by a multiple-feed mechanical oiler. The engine was turned over by means of a unique ratchet starting system. Rated at 20 drawbar and 40 belt hp, the engine proved extremely reliable. The transmission of the 20/40 offered two forward and one reverse speed. As with the 30/60, the drive gears were exposed.

A number of changes were made to the 20/40 over the course of production. As mentioned, engine displacement was increased twice. Other revisions to the 20/40 engine included a different style of intake manifold that repositioned the carburetor below the level of the fuel tanks, thereby improving the fuel feed to the engine.

Starting a Model 30/60
Starting a Case Model 30/60 was a Herculean task. This thresherman pulls on the giant exposed flywheel to turn the engine in the hope of getting it started. (Photograph © by Dave Arnold)

The original cooling system featured a tubular-type radiator and cooling tank that relied on induced draft to pull air through the radiator. Unlike the 30/60, however, there was no water pump. Rather, circulation was dependent on thermo siphoning, or the natural tendency for warm water to circulate continuously through a closed system. In 1916, a cell-type radiator with upper and lower holding tanks replaced the original tubular-type, and the induced draft system was augmented by a fan that was driven off the engine flywheel.

On earlier 20/40s the operator platform was carried on top of the channel-iron chassis. On later units it was placed between the chassis side members. Consequently, the cab of later units was positioned lower than that of earlier units.

The 20/40 was promoted as a five- to six-plow tractor. Weighing almost 14,000 pounds (6,300 kg), it too was considered a heavyweight tractor. Its reputation for reliability boosted the market for Case gas tractors and further diminished the market for steam.

The Mammoth Model 40/80 of 1913

In October 1913, the Case board approved construction of one hundred 80-hp tractors. The design featured a horizontal four-cylinder engine placed on the chassis of the Case 30/60. The largest of the Case heavyweight gas tractors, only two are known to have been built. No more information is available about these tractors, and other than the photos of the engine appearing exclusively in this book, no photographs of either tractor exist.

Case most likely did not build the engine for the 40/80, as there are no records to indicate production of such a horizontal four-cylinder engine. However, Minneapolis Steel & Machinery Company did build comparable engines. As this firm also built the chassis for the 30/60, it likely supplied Case with the engine depicted in the photographs.

Case's First Small Tractor: Model 12/25 of 1913–1918

Although neither as heavy as their steam counterparts, nor as expensive to buy and operate, gasoline tractors such as the 30/60 and 20/40 were nevertheless cumbersome and costly. Before the debut of Henry Ford's Fordson from Dearborn, Michigan, few but the most successful farmers could afford a new tractor. Yet from the earliest days of power farming, enthusiasm and demand for tractors was universal. Manufacturers realized that smaller and less-expensive tractors were required to meet demand. Beginning about 1912, a number of smaller tractors emerged and met with great acceptance. Case also rushed to build smaller tractors, the first of which was the Model 12/25.

The Model 12/25 was introduced in 1913 and built through 1918. The 12/25 featured a two-cylinder horizontal opposed engine of 6½x7-inch (162.5x175-mm) bore and stroke, which was later increased to 7x7 inches (175x175 mm). Equipped with Kingston carburetors and magnetos, the engine was cooled by thermo siphoning and fan. The transmission offered two forward speeds.

The 12/25 was a sleek-looking tractor for its day, with an open operator platform, a low profile, and an enclosed engine compartment. Weighing almost 9,000 pounds (4,050 kg), it was 5,000 pounds (2,250 kg) lighter than the 20/40. Rated as a four-plow tractor, the 12/25 won a gold medal for drawbar performance at the 1914 Winnipeg trials.

Model 30/60
The engine of the 30/60 was a horizontal two-cylinder of 10x12-inch (250x300-mm) bore and stroke. The engine fathered 30–35 drawbar hp and 60 belt hp. The tractor weighed a mammoth 25,800 pounds (11,610 kg). The price for this state-of-the-art gas tractor was $2,500 in 1912 and $2,800 in 1914. This 1912 Case Model 30/60 was displayed at the 1989 Rollag, Minnesota, threshing show. (Photograph © by Dave Arnold)

Model 30/60 Frame, circa 1910s
The frame of the 30/60 was built up from 10-inch (25-cm) channel steel. As with most tractors of the day, the transmission gearing was exposed to the elements. At the rear, the smaller of two tanks held 11 gallons (42 liters) of gasoline; the larger carried 26 gallons (99 liters) of kerosene. The ill-fated Model 40/80 was built using the same frame.

Grabbing the Little Bull by the Horns: Model 10/20 of 1915–1918

The best-selling gas tractor of 1913 and 1914 was the Little Bull, built by the Bull Tractor Company of Minneapolis. The Little Bull was a 3,800-pound (1,710-kg), 12-hp three-wheel tractor. Priced at $335—a quarter of the price of the Case 12/25—the Little Bull was not particularly well designed nor was it adequately powered. Yet it sold, proving that farmers hungered for a small, low-priced tractor. The success of the Little Bull spawned a number of imitators, all of which were low-cost, lightweight three-wheelers. Case grabbed the Little Bull by the horns and offered its Model 10/20.

Introduced in 1915, the Model 10/20 became the best-selling Case gas tractor of this early period, with sales eventually topping 6,600 units. It featured an automotive-type, vertical four-cylinder engine of 4¼x6-inch (106x150-mm) bore and stroke, that developed 20 belt hp at 900 rpm. Equipped with a Kingston carburetor and magneto, the engine was cooled by means of a pump and fan.

Although it sold well, the 10/20 was not a particularly well-designed tractor. It offered one wheel in front and only one tractive wheel in the rear. A second, narrower rear wheel served as an outrigger. The simple design did not require a differential; instead, a special "jaw clutch" transferred power to both wheels to give additional traction, if required. The tractor suffered from relatively feeble drawbar pull. Visibility to the front was poor since the operator sat in a low position at the rear of the tractor. Nonetheless, the 10/20 was a move in the right direction—a lightweight, smaller tractor, targeted at the average farmer.

Model 30/60 Transmission, circa 1910s
The drive gears of the Model 30/60 viewed from the differential side.

Case Automobiles

Following the advent of the newfangled horseless carriage at the turn of the century, the expanding Case company soon jumped onto the bandwagon. In 1910, Case purchased the small Pierce Motor Company of Racine, which bore no connection with the large and famous Pierce-Arrow. Case soon started building high-quality automobiles in the luxury class. In 1911, three Case racing cars were entered in the first Indianapolis 500 race, occupying the pole position and two spots in the second row, although they failed to win the race.

Case's 1917 farming catalog included a pitch for the firm's Model 40 Touring Car that was ripe with glowing prose and a pioneering vision of a bountiful future:

In this day of big production in the motor car industry buyers are making very careful comparisons in choosing motor cars. And this is only to be expected for big quantity production has dominated the organizations of many makers. Quality has been sacrificed and relegated to the background. So when you are about to enjoy the endless and joyous comforts of the automobile, your money should find its way to the car that you know and that you are certain will guarantee to you maximum service for the money spent. Place quality uppermost in your mind when buying. Consider the Company behind the product. Such a comparison will naturally decide you in favor of the Case 40.

"Not how many, but how good," is the spirit of the Case organization. "Quality cars only" is our aim. In the 1917 Case 40 a thorough investigation will reveal a host of things well done. All over the country people will stop to admire its clean cut beauty. The Case method of suspending the cantilever springs from the rear axle makes a car of unusual and delightful comfort. You, of course, will appreciate this feature, but to your wife it will be doubly appreciative. Ample room in the tonneau and front compartment makes it appeal to the entire family. Nothing is left undone to make this car a masterpiece.

This car marks a new standard in automobile values. It is the car of cars.

The tractor had been a mechanical substitute for Old Dobbin, and ate gas instead of hay. But the general-purpose tractor, with its power take-off, planted, cultivated and harvested. It practically wiped out the 'doubtful' and 'non-tractor' operations listed in 1921.
—*Prairie Farmer*, 1941

Case Touring Car
When the horseless carriage made its debut, J. I. Case was quick to try its hand at building an automobile of its own. This 1917 Case touring car featured a Case four-cylinder L-head engine that fathered 40–45 hp. The wheels were made of wood in the typical "artillery style" of the era. This Case automobile was displayed at the Rough and Tumble Thrashers Show in Kinzers, Pennsylvania, in 1989. (Photograph © by Dave Arnold)

ABOVE: Model 20/40
The engine of the 20/40 was a horizontal, opposed two-cylinder with 8¼x9-inch (206x225-mm) bore and stroke. The engine created 20–25 drawbar hp and 40 belt hp. The 20/40 cost $2,000 in 1915 and $2,500 in 1920. (Photograph © by Dave Arnold)

RIGHT: Model 20/40, 1917
In the back of its grand 1917 catalog behind the listings of steamers, Case detailed its recently released line of gas and oil tractors, including the 20/40.

Case 20-40 Tractor

ABOVE: Model 20/40 Still at Work, 1948
The Model 20/40 gas and kerosene tractor was noted for its durability and performance, day in and day out. This 1912 Model 20/40 was still at work when this photo was taken in 1948.

LEFT: Model 20/40, circa 1910s
Case boasted that its Model 20/40 was "A Tractor That Has 'Made Good.'" The Model 20/40 is a classic example of Case engineering at its best. Its two-cylinder opposed engine and two-speed transmission were noted for durability and reliability.

ABOVE: Model 20/40
The later version of the Case Model 20/40 gas tractor featured this redesigned radiator and added a fan for forced induction of cooling air. (Photograph © by Dave Arnold)

RIGHT: Model 20/40
The early version of the Case Model 20/40 gas tractor featured this square radiator mounted with the tubular exhaust. Early units used thermosiphon cooling circulation that induced a draft through the radiator created by engine exhaust as it discharged up through the stack on top of the radiator. (Photograph © by Dave Arnold)

ABOVE: Model 40/80 Engine, 1913
No photographs of the Model 40/80 are known to exist, but the description on the back of this Case archive photo identified the subject as the "motor for 80 gas tractor." Dated August 1913, the photograph shows the four connecting rods, crankshaft, and camshaft. The mechanical oiler and its plumbing are in plain view.

LEFT: Model 40/80 Engine, 1913
This view from the top of the cylinders shows the carburetor and manifolds of the 80-hp horizontal motor. Note Old Abe, the Case eagle, cast into the exhaust manifold.

Model 10/20 at Work, 1916
A big seller—but hardly the best example of Case engineering—the Model 10/20 was the Case response to the Little Bull, a three-wheeler and the best-selling tractor of 1914. Forward vision on the 10/20 was restricted. The operator sat low and at the far right; he could see neither the front wheel nor the left side of the tractor. This 10/20 pulls two Case binders while harvesting a field of oats.

Model 10/20
The 10/20 was powered by a vertical four-cylinder engine of 4¼x6 inches (106x150 mm) bore and stroke. It produced 10–12 drawbar hp and 20 belt hp. This unrestored, original case Model 10/20 was on display at the 1989 Rough and Tumble Thrashers Show in Kinzers, Pennsylvania. (Photograph © by Dave Arnold)

RIGHT: Model 10/20, circa 1910s
Ads such as this touted the 10/20 as a dependable, all-purpose machine. Despite its weaknesses, the 10/20 outsold the 12/25 two to one. Granted, the last of the 10/20s remained in Case inventory until 1924!

RIGHT, TOP: Model 30/60
*One of a handful of Case Model 30/60s
that has survived the decades, this machine was photographed at the Western
Minnesota Steam Threshers Reunion
held in Rollag, Minnesota.*

RIGHT, BOTTOM: Model 20/40, 1912
*A very early Model 20/40 pulling a four-
bottom plow. The best-selling Case
heavyweight, the 20/40 was built from
1912 through 1919.*

BELOW: Model 10/20 Ad, circa 1910s
*Advertising its Model 10/20 as "the most
popular in its class" was stretching the
truth a bit. Case developed the 10/20 as
a response the best-selling Little Bull
tractor.*

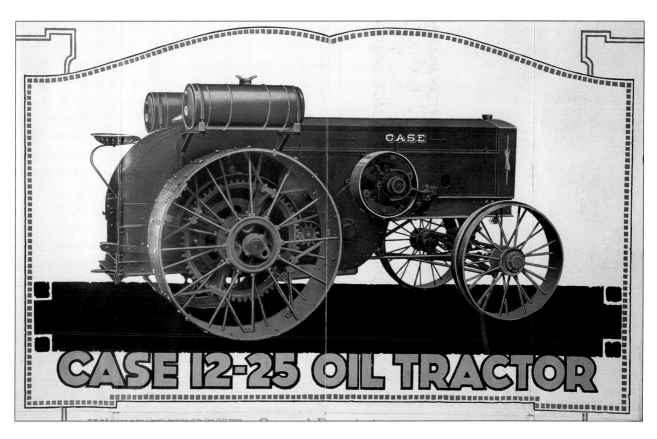

CASE 12-25 OIL TRACTOR

ABOVE: Model 12/25, circa 1910s
With its long hood and engine side panels, the Model 12/25 presented a sleek silhouette. At 9,000 pounds (4,050 kg), the 12/25 was neither a heavyweight nor a lightweight. Case claimed it would easily pull a four-bottom plow or drive a 26x46-inch (65x115-cm) thresher.

LEFT: Model 20/40
The 20/40 was a lightweight tractor for its age: it weighed a mere 13,700 pounds (6,165 kg). This 1915 Case Model 20/40 is owned by Clifford Vangsness. (Photograph © by Dave Arnold)

The light tractor has made tractor farming possible for countless numbers of small farmers.
—*Capper's Farmer, 1935*

YOU NEED ONE OF THESE OUTFITS FOR

22-40 H. P.

15-27 H. P.

Case 22-40 H. P. Kerosene Tractor
Grand Detour Self-Lift — 4-Furrow — Power Plow

An ideal outfit for the careful farmer who wants to avoid undue soil packing with heavy tractors and at the same time sees the necessity for sufficient power to drive the larger Thresher, Silo Filler and other heavy-duty belt driven equipment. Where large belt driven machinery and extensive acreage combine to make a tractor of this size especially adaptable, the purchaser will find this Case 22-40 H. P. Kerosene Tractor very profitable to own.

Case 15-27 H. P. Kerosene Tractor
Grand Detour Self-Lift — 3-Furrow — Power Plow

With sufficient power to meet the requirements of a fully equipped 26x46 Case Thresher or pulling three 14" plows easily under all ordinary conditions, what tractor could be of greater general use to the average farmer? All Case tractors have powerful, valve-in-head motors with liberal reserve power over their rating, and all cut steel, spur gears, enclosed and running in oil. They can deliver full rated H. P. on gasoline, kerosene or distillate without overheating.

NOTICE *We want the public to know that our plows and harrows are NOT the Case plows and harrows made by the*

J. I. CASE THRESHING MACHINE COMPANY, Inc., RACINE, W

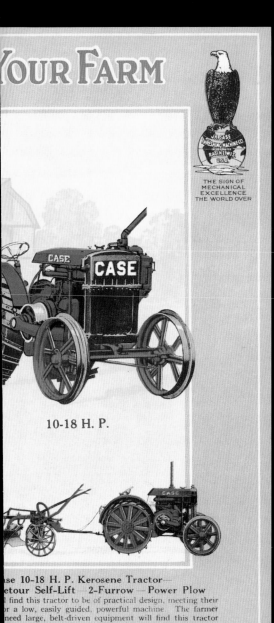

YOUR FARM

THE SIGN OF
MECHANICAL
EXCELLENCE
THE WORLD OVER

10-18 H. P.

...ase 10-18 H. P. Kerosene Tractor—
...etour Self-Lift—2-Furrow—Power Plow
...l find this tractor to be of practical design, meeting their
...r a low, easily guided, powerful machine. The farmer
...need large, belt-driven equipment will find this tractor
...reparing seed beds, harvesting and threshing.
...Lift Power Plows of the rigid beam type come in 2—3—4—5 bottom
...or 14" bottoms. We furnish mould board shapes to meet soil conditions
...ndent beam plows can be furnished in 3—4—5 and 6 bottom gangs.

...Plow Works Co.
...U. S. A.

The Great Crossmotors

Case's Famous Four-Cylinder Tractors, 1915–1928

Do your work the power way. It will save time and labor, takes off the heavy burdens of farming. A Case tractor is built to give continuous service, day and night if necessary, never tires. When not in use, requires no attention, doesn't eat when idle. Seventy-five thousand farmers are power farming because it is the profitable way and the easy, modern way.
—Case catalog, 1910s

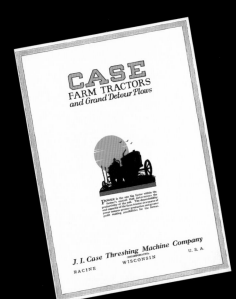

Work on the next generation of Case gas tractors began in late 1915, by which time the industry was producing a variety of lightweight gas tractors in the two-to-four-plow category. It was critical that Case follow suit, as sales of steam tractors were declining rapidly.

In 1915, Case introduced the first of its legendary four-cylinder Crossmotor tractors, a highly competitive series that assured Case a position as a leader in the gas-tractor marketplace.

Model 9/18 of 1917–1918

The Model 9/18 featured a transverse-mounted, vertical four-cylinder engine, with 3⅞x5-inch (97x125-mm) bore and stroke. The tractor frame was built up from 5-inch (125-mm) steel channel. A sloping hood and side panels enclosed the engine. The short wheelbase carried a fully enclosed two-speed transmission and running gear. The 9/18 also introduced the Case Air Washer, a patented air cleaner system that drew air through a water-filled canister and filter.

Built for only the two years, the 9/18 and its successors were promoted as two-plow tractors.

Model 9/18B and Model 10/18 of 1918–1922

In 1918, Case introduced a successor to the 9/18, the Model 9/18B. The new tractor differed in one significant regard: it featured a one-piece cast-iron frame that replaced the structural steel frame of the 9/18. This lightweight but strong chassis integrated the front axle support, engine crankcase and transmission, and rear axle housings in one unit. The upper half of the engine was bolted directly to the frame, with an oil pan bolted beneath the frame. Other small changes included the replacement of the sloping hood with a level hood; elimination of engine side panels; and flat wheel spokes in place of the earlier round ones.

The Model 10/18 succeeded the 9/18B, apparently within the same year. The 10/18's crankshaft was heavier than the 9/18B's, its engine speed increased from 900 to 1,050 rpm, and its drawbar horsepower output was boosted slightly. The 10/18 also introduced a new thermostatically controlled cooling system and full-pressure feed-type engine lubrication, with a drilled crankshaft to feed oil to the bearings.

The 9/18, 9/18B, and 10/18 were rated as two-plow tractors. Besides agricultural versions, industrial tractors were offered equipped with solid rubber tires.

There is some confusion as to the number of each model built. Total production for the three models approached 15,000 units by the time 10/18 production ceased in 1921.

Model 12/20 of 1922–1928

In 1922, the Model 12/20 succeeded the Model 10/18. It was re-designated the Model A in 1928.

The 12/20 was not simply a re-rated version of the 10/18. Engine displacement was increased to 4⅛x5 inches (103x125 mm), and the crankshaft was carried on three main bearings rather than two. Output was

Case Dealer Sign, circa 1920
The Case dealer catalog offered this dazzling dealer sign in the 1920s.

increased from 18 to 25 hp. Overall length of the tractor was 7½ inches (187.5 mm) greater, and it weighed nearly 700 pounds (315 kg) more.

The 12/20 featured a rather complex exhaust manifold that was designed to improve fuel economy by preheating air in the intake manifold featuring what Case termed "exhaust deflectors." Controlled by levers, the deflectors were placed on either end of the manifold. Turning them horizontally allowed exhaust gases from all four cylinders to pass around the intake manifold and raise air temperature in the manifold. Turning the levers straight up allowed the exhaust from the end cylinders to go through a bypass to the main exhaust without coming in contact with the intake manifold.

The 12/20 also featured a Case Air Washer and water feed valve that worked to dampen pre-ignition. This system required careful regulation by the operator. The 12/20 is easily distinguished by its unique stamped-steel wheels that appear to be flat spokes.

Overall performance of the 12/20 made it popular in both farm and industrial applications, and over the years, Case sold nearly 12,000 units.

Models 15/27, 18/32, and K of 1919–1927

The Model 15/27 and its successors the Model 18/32 and Model K were the best-selling models of the Crossmotors. By 1927, Case sold over 27,000 units of the 15/27, 18/32, and Model K combined. Virtually identical, the versions differed, however, in horsepower output.

The basic construction of the 15/27 was similar to that of the 10/18 and 12/20, but built on a larger scale. The 15/27 featured a transverse or cross-mounted four-cylinder engine with 4½x6-inch (112.5x150-mm) bore and stroke riding on a rigid, cast-iron frame. The transmission and final drives were fully enclosed with two forward speeds.

The 15/27 was rated as a four-plow tractor. The engine generated 31.23 maximum belt and 18.8 maximum drawbar hp in its Nebraska test. Drawbar pull was 3,440 pounds (1,548 kg).

The 18/32, with a higher-rated engine speed than the 15/27, developed 36.73 maximum belt and 24.01 maximum drawbar hp in its Nebraska test.

Models 22/40, 25/45, and T of 1919–1928

Although not the biggest of the Crossmotors, the 22/40 was a low-production tractor suited to the needs of bigger farms. Rated to handle five plows, its four-cylinder engine, with cylinders cast in pairs, generated a maximum 40.16 engine and 29.04 drawbar hp. Bore and stroke measured 5½x6¾ inches (137.5x169 mm).

The 22/40 weighed over 9,900 pounds (4,455 kg)—hardly a lightweight tractor. Its frame was constructed from 7- and 8-inch (175- and 200-mm) sections of channel steel and boiler plate, rather than cast iron. The transmission gears were carried in a cast-iron case, and the final drives were fully enclosed.

The 25/45 and Model T differed only slightly from the 22/40 yet their performances were significantly improved over the lower-powered

Model 9/18 Ad, circa 1910s
Case advertised its kerosene tractors as being "Preferred By Most Progressive Farmers."

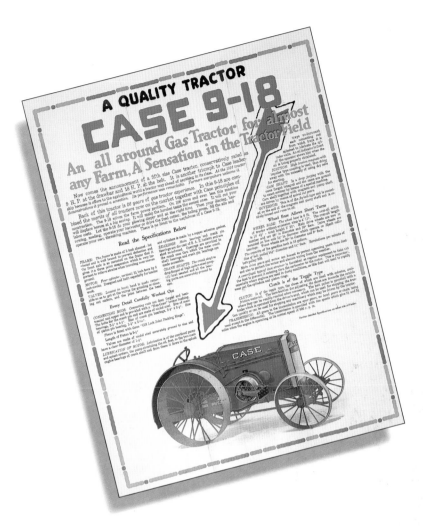

ABOVE: Model 9/18, circa 1910s
Case claimed that there was no limit to the usefulness of a 9/18.

FACING PAGE, TOP: Model 9/18B Powering Thresher, 1917
The 9/18B replaced the 9/18. Its life was brief, however, as it was soon succeeded by the Model 10/18. The 9/18B featured a cast-iron main frame rather than the channel-iron frame of the 9/18. This unit was photographed in August 1917 on the farm of Stephen Bull, brother-in-law of J. I. Case.

FACING PAGE, INSET: Model 9/18 and Grader, 1917
The Case 9/18 Crossmotor tractor was promoted as suitable for a farm of 100 acres (40 hectares) or less. It also found work as an industrial tractor, such as pulling this Case road grader in Racine, Wisconsin.

tractor. In its Nebraska test, the 25/45 produced 45.18 engine and 32.96 drawbar hp. Drawbar pull jumped from the 4,965 pounds (2,234 kg) of the 22/40 to 5,750 pounds (2,588 kg) of the 25/45.

Case built fewer than 2,500 tractors of this series. Priced at more than twice the cost of the 18/32, this series was undoubtedly targeted at the farmer who sought to replace an earlier heavyweight machine.

A New Generation of Heavyweight: Model 40/72 of 1920–1923

For whatever the reason, Case saw fit to manufacture the Model 40/72. At the time when Henry Ford swept the nation with his lightweight Fordson and International Harvester of Chicago worked to develop the first general-purpose tractor in its Farmall, Case built a "new generation" ultra-heavyweight tractor.

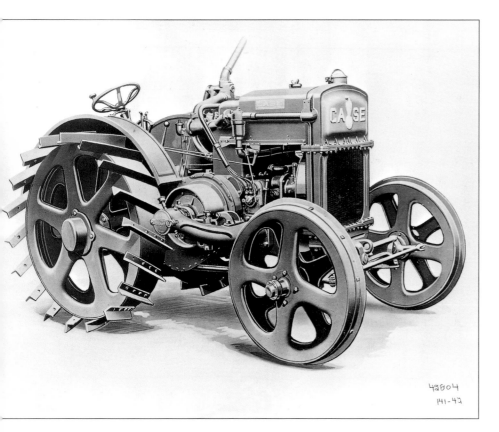

The largest of the Crossmotors, the 40/72 weighed 22,000 pounds (9,900 kg) and stood more than nine feet (270 cm) tall. Its four-cylinder, 7x8-inch (175x200-mm) engine produced over 90 hp. Rated as an eight-to-twelve-plow tractor, the 40/72 produced 10,886 pounds (4,900 kg) drawbar pull in its Nebraska test.

Construction of the 40/72 was similar to that of the 22/40. It was supported by a heavy frame built up of 8- and 10-inch (200- and 250-mm) sections of steel channel and boiler plate. Its four-cylinder engine featured cylinders cast in pairs, and the two-speed transmission boasted fully enclosed final drives.

Promoted for both farm and road construction applications, Case built only forty-one units.

ABOVE, TOP: Model 10/18, 1918
The stocky appearance of the Model 10/18 was typical of the Case Crossmotors. The 10/18 provided adequate power to pull a two-bottom plow or 8-foot (240-cm) double-sided disk.

ABOVE, BOTTOM: Model 12/20, 1918
The broad-spoke wheels of the Model 12/20 distinguished it from the rest of the Crossmotor series. The complex manifold and air washer system of the 12/20 (also used on larger Crossmotor models) diverted hot exhaust gases around the intake manifold. The elevated temperature supposedly improved combustion. Whether or not it was effective is irrelevant today, as corrosion has taken its toll, and few tractors remain with the original system intact.

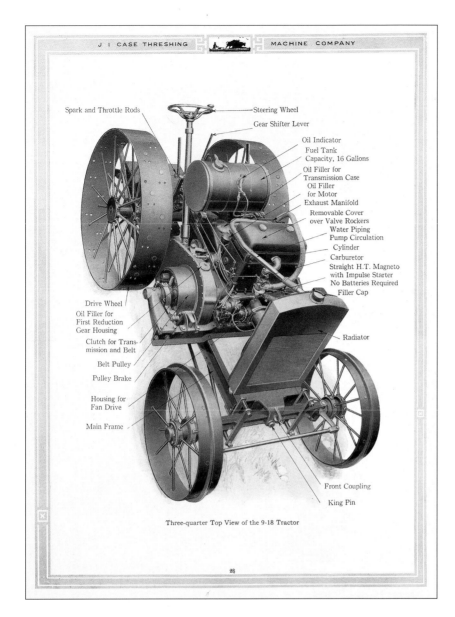

Spark and Throttle Rods

Steering Wheel

Gear Shifter Lever

Oil Indicator

Fuel Tank
Capacity, 16 Gallons

Oil Filler for
Transmission Case

Oil Filler
for Motor

Exhaust Manifold

Removable Cover
over Valve Rockers

Water Piping
Pump Circulation

Cylinder

Carburetor

Straight H.T. Magneto
with Impulse Starter
No Batteries Required

Filler Cap

Drive Wheel

Oil Filler for
First Reduction
Gear Housing

Clutch for Trans-
mission and Belt

Belt Pulley

Pulley Brake

Housing for
Fan Drive

Main Frame

Radiator

Front Coupling

King Pin

Three-quarter Top View of the 9-18 Tractor

26

*There is a baffling array of
machinery, each separate con-
trivance performing its ingenious
function, cutting labor costs and
raising the vocation of the farmer
from the slavish drudgery of the
days of peasant serfdom to
the dignity of a scientific or
professional calling.*
—Barton W. Currie,
The Tractor, 1916

Model 9/18 Details, 1917
*The 1917 catalog showed the technical
details of the 9/18 model.*

Case Logo
*Case's name stood out in large, bold type
cast into the radiator shroud of its
Crossmotor tractors.* (Photograph © by
Dave Arnold)

514-K.T.

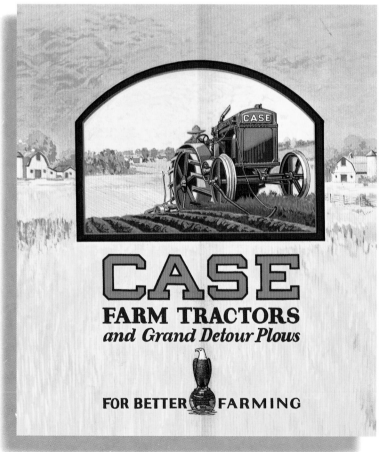

CASE
FARM TRACTORS
and Grand Detour Plows

FOR BETTER FARMING

ABOVE: Model 15/27, 1919
The 15/27 was the best selling of the Case Crossmotors. Equipped with hard rubber tires, this unit was undoubtedly used in an industrial application. Available as industrial and standard farm models, the 15/27 and its successor the 18/32 were also offered in road, orchard, and rice versions.

LEFT: Case Catalog with Crossmotor, circa 1920
A Case Crossmotor crests a hill while plowing, with visions of a bountiful harvest in the background.

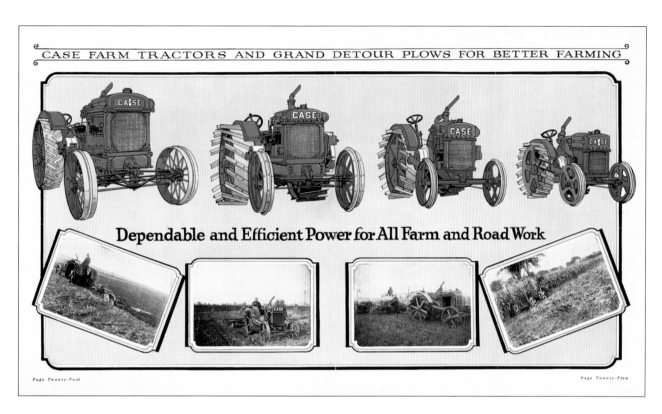

Dependable and Efficient Power for All Farm and Road Work

Page Twenty-Four

Page Twenty-Five

ABOVE: Crossmotor Lineup, circa 1920
Case's lineup of Crossmotors included from right, the 12/20 with its distinctive wheels, 15/27, 22/40, and monster 40/72.

LEFT: Case Catalog with Crossmotor
Case promised "Better Farming With Better Tractors." By the dawn of the 1920s, the firm's catalog was focused on its Crossmotor models in 12/20, 15/27, and 22/40 ratings.

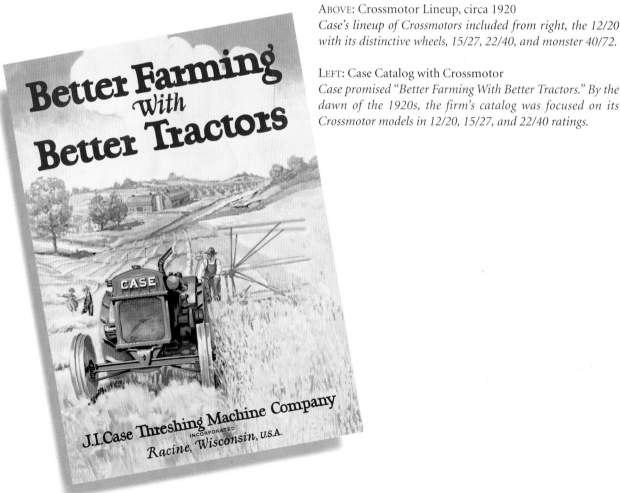

55

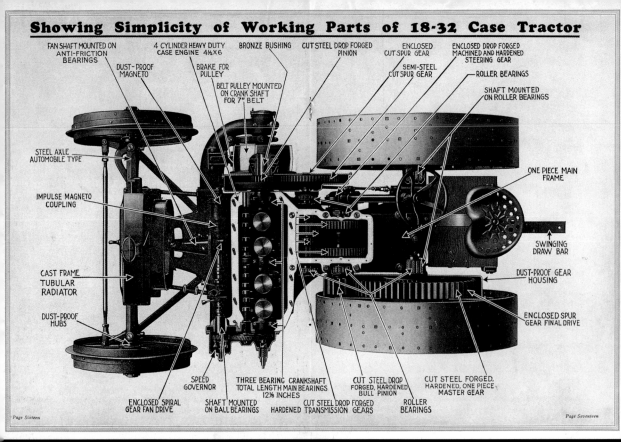

Showing Simplicity of Working Parts of 18-32 Case Tractor

FAN SHAFT MOUNTED ON ANTI-FRICTION BEARINGS

DUST-PROOF MAGNETO

4 CYLINDER HEAVY DUTY CASE ENGINE 4½x6

BRAKE FOR PULLEY

BRONZE BUSHING

CUT STEEL DROP FORGED PINION

ENCLOSED CUT SPUR GEAR

ENCLOSED DROP FORGED MACHINED AND HARDENED STEERING GEAR

SEMI-STEEL CUT SPUR GEAR

ROLLER BEARINGS

BELT PULLEY MOUNTED ON CRANK SHAFT FOR 7" BELT

SHAFT MOUNTED ON ROLLER BEARINGS

STEEL AXLE AUTOMOBILE TYPE

IMPULSE MAGNETO COUPLING

ONE PIECE MAIN FRAME

SWINGING DRAW BAR

CAST FRAME TUBULAR RADIATOR

DUST-PROOF GEAR HOUSING

DUST-PROOF HUBS

ENCLOSED SPUR GEAR FINAL DRIVE

SPEED GOVERNOR

THREE BEARING CRANKSHAFT TOTAL LENGTH MAIN BEARINGS 12⅛ INCHES

CUT STEEL DROP FORGED, HARDENED BULL PINION

CUT STEEL FORGED, HARDENED, ONE PIECE MASTER GEAR

ENCLOSED SPIRAL GEAR FAN DRIVE

SHAFT MOUNTED ON BALL BEARINGS

CUT STEEL DROP FORGED HARDENED TRANSMISSION GEARS

ROLLER BEARINGS

ABOVE: Crossmotor Layout
As can be seen in this overhead view of the 18/32 frame, the engine crankcase and transmission housing were an integral part of the cast-iron main frame.

RIGHT: Model 22/40, circa 1920
The 22/40 and its successor the 25/45 were five-plow tractors built for rugged duty. Weighing nearly five tons (4,500 kg), the frame was built from 7- and 8-inch (17.5- and 20-cm) channel steel and boiler plate. Unlike the four-cylinder monobloc engine of the smaller Crossmotor tractors, the engine of the 22/40 and 25/45 featured four cylinders cast in pairs with individual cylinder heads.

BETTER FARMING

The Case 22-40 Farm Tractor

THE Case 22-40 is especially suited to the requirements of the farmer with large acreage, or one who has a great deal of belt work to do, such as threshing or filling silos. It has enough power to handle custom jobs efficiently and its economy makes it a profitable tractor for such work. It is an ideal power unit for the contractor who wants efficient and dependable power for road work, hauling, breaking land, and other profitable operations.

Usefulness   In plowing ordinary ground it will pull five 14-inch bottoms. In heavy ground and breaking it will handle four bottoms easily. One man can thus turn over at least twice as much ground in a day as he would with a two plow tractor and with considerably less fuel per acre.

It will handle two 8-foot tandem disk harrows; three grain binders; two 12-foot grain drills and a 24-foot drag, or any other combination of implements requiring between 12 and 15 horses.

It will handle a 32x54 thresher with attachments in ordinary threshing, a 20-inch silo filler, or any belt machine requiring 40 H.P. or less to operate.

It is exceptionally well adapted for road work and hauling of all kinds.

Some of the advantages of this tractor for this kind of work are:

Two forward speeds, 2-1/5 and 3-1/5 miles per hour are provided. These have been found the most desirable speeds for the work a tractor of this size has to do.

Special Road Speed   The 22-40 tractor can be equipped with a special high road speed of 4 miles per hour for road work.

Proper distribution of weight together with well designed grouters assure maximum traction in

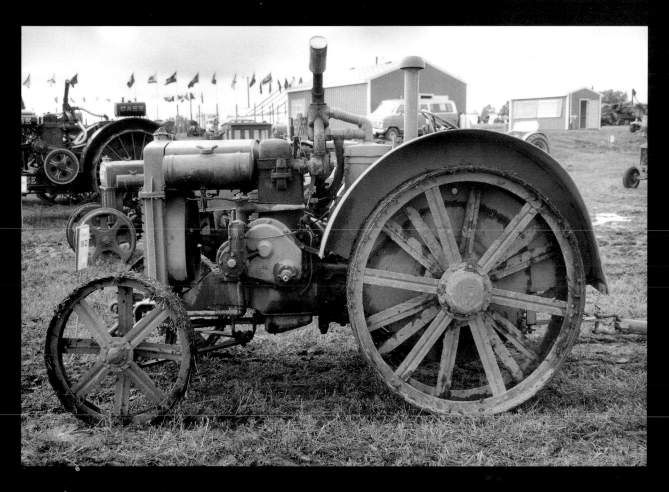

Above: Model 18/32
The 18/32 was a re-rated 15/27 that developed 5 hp more at the drawbar. The 18/32 engine operated at 1,000 rpm versus 900 rpm for the 15/27. Otherwise the tractors were virtually identical.

Left: Case Logo
(Photograph © by Dave Arnold)

ABOVE: Case 12/20 and LA
Good restoration material: On the left is a 12/20 Crossmotor, while on the right is a 1950s vintage Model LA. (Photograph © by Dave Arnold)

LEFT: Case Combine Catalog with Crossmotor, circa 1920s
Case always promoted its full line of farming equipment.

FACING PAGE: Case Catalog with Crossmotor, circa 1921
On this catalog back cover, Case boasted of all the possible tasks the Crossmotor tractor could accomplish.

PLOWING WITH A CASE TRACTOR

SEEDING WITH A CASE TRACTOR

HARVESTING WITH A CASE TRACTOR

FILLING SILO WITH A CASE TRACTOR

PULVERIZING WITH A CASE TRACTOR

THRESHING WITH A CASE OUTFIT

THE SIGN OF MECHANICAL EXCELLENCE THE WORLD OVER

J.I. CASE THRESHING MACHINE CO. INC.
RACINE, WISCONSIN, U.S.A.

*A Million Farmer-Engineers as
Our Advisors.*
—Case ad, 1918

ABOVE, TOP: Model 40/72
*The engine of the 40/72 was a vertical, four-cylinder of 7x8-inch
(175x200-mm) bore and stroke. It fathered 40 drawbar hp and 72
belt hp.* (Photograph © by Dave Arnold)

ABOVE, BOTTOM: Model 40/72
*The 40/72 weighed a mammoth 21,200 pounds (9,540 kg). It cost
$4,000 in 1923.* (Photograph © by Dave Arnold)

LEFT: Case Catalog with Crossmotor

CASE ROAD TRACTORS ✦ FOUR STANDARD SIZES

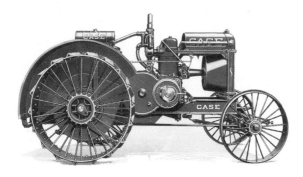

The Case 40-72 Tractor For Road Work

CAPABLE of exerting a drawbar pull of 12,000 lbs., (maximum) and delivering over 90 brake horse power (maximum) for belt work, the 40-72 Case road tractor has as great a capacity for work as we believe practical to build in one unit. It weighs 21,200 lbs., and the wheelbase is only 124 inches. Undoubtedly, this tractor stands alone as a large power unit of the most advanced type of design and construction. It affords contractors many advantages in carrying on large projects because of an adaptability for practically all work encountered in extensive road construction.

The 40-72 possesses features giving it durability and dependability beyond that of other tractors of similar size. As for economy, it is unsurpassed first because of the fuel efficiency obtained through proper design and finally because of the greater amount of work done in a given time due to the ease with which the 40-72 can be operated on drawbar as well as belt work. It is a new development—with all the modern improvements devised by some of the most skilled American engineers. In the two years these machines have been in general use, they have proved the value of Case experience extending over a period of 80 years. To any contractors with big work to do, the 40-72 offers remarkable possibilities for increased profit.

Page Twelve

PROFITABLE USES FOR THE 40-72

The Case 40-72 tractor can be used profitably for road work because it is able to move large volumes of dirt, and other road building materials at the very minimum cost per yard. This holds true for hauling, blade grading and operating elevating graders. It will do any of this work at least 50 per cent cheaper than it can be done with horses. Not only that, it can do road work faster, and do it much better. Further than this the 40-72 tractor is capable of doing work that cannot be done with horses and that is beyond the ability of tractors with less power.

In grading with a 12-foot grader and back sloper, the power of the 40-72 is adequate for the full use of this machine. The big advantage lies in the abundance of power at hand to move a full blade of dirt to the center of the road. The tractor travels in the center of the road at all times, where it packs the loose dirt and provides a hard road bed at once. The 40-72 provides power for making the kind of road side ditches, usually specified, in few operations, at correspondingly decreased cost. Other types of power and smaller tractors have to be attached directly at the front of the grader and so work at considerable disadvantage.

ABOVE: Model 40/72
The largest tractor in Case's Crossmotor range, the Model 40/72 weighed some 22,000 pounds (9,900 kg). (Photograph © by Dave Arnold)

LEFT: Model 40/72, 1920
The largest of all Crossmotors, the 40/72 could handle a 12-foot (360-cm) grader or an eight- to twelve-bottom plow with ease.

Illinois Farmers Vote Six to One for Tractor Farming.
—*Prairie Farmer* headline, 1918

Chapter 5

The Pioneering General-Purpose Tractors

The Gray Era, 1929–1940

Modern farming demands lower farming costs. Changing soil, weather and crop conditions, faster roads from farm to market, wider uses for tractor power on drawbar, belt and power takeoff, have resulted in greater and increased demands on the time, labor and money-saving ability of tractors. In all sorts of situations, Case tractors successfully cut costs in every way.
—Case catalog, 1930s

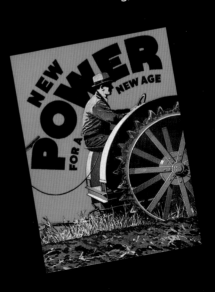

LEFT: Model RC
A 1936 Model RC owned by Tim Reynolds of Rock Creek, Minnesota. (Photograph
© by Dave Arnold)

Sales of the Crossmotors were on the increase in the late 1920s. Yet with the debut of the unitized construction of the Fordson and the trim, sturdy design of the three-speed, general-purpose Farmall, Case's tractors suddenly seemed outdated. Their broad-framed stocky appearance, transverse-mounted engines, and two-speed transmissions had limited appeal to the modern farmers.

By late 1925, Case recognized the developments and changes taking place within the industry and took steps to develop a new series of tractors. Prototypes were in the field by the spring of 1928, and production of the Model L and Model C followed in 1929.

Model CC Ad, circa 1930s

The Start of a New Era: Model L of 1929–1939

The Model L and its smaller companion the Model C were well-designed tractors with certain characteristics that influenced the design of subsequent Case models well into the 1960s.

The first Case tractor to feature unitized construction, the L offered a new four-cylinder engine, a new three-speed transmission, and a roller-chain final drive. The engine was cast *en bloc*. It offered renewable cylinder sleeves, a three-main-bearing crankshaft, a more simplified exhaust manifold from that fitted to the Crossmotor series, and an oil-bath air cleaner. The three-forward-speed transmission featured a hand-operated clutch.

The L was also built as an industrial tractor, designated the Model LI. Although Case had also promoted and sold the Crossmotor series as industrial tractors, there was little to differentiate an industrial Crossmotor model from an agricultural version. The LI, on the other hand, offered some distinctively different features from the Model L: a foot-operated clutch, hand and foot throttles, heavy-duty front axle, solid or pneumatic tires, and in later models, an optional four-speed transmission.

A solid three-plow tractor and modern in every respect, the Model L handily outsold its Crossmotor predecessors. The L remained in production for ten years, during which time factory cabs, electric starters and lights, rubber tires, and high-speed gearing for increased road speed were added as options.

The Smaller Sibling: Model C of 1929–1939

The Model C, introduced within months of the Model L, was virtually identical to the L but built on a smaller scale. Engine, transmission, and final-drive characteristics were therefore similar. The standard Model C was rated as a two-plow tractor, whereas the L ably handled three 14-inch (35-cm) plow bottoms.

The Model C was built in a variety of configurations. Most notable was the Model CC, the first Case general-purpose or row-crop tractor. The overwhelming success of the Farmall had spawned dozens of imitators, the Model CC among them. The advantages of the row-crop tractor—greater ground clearance, adjustable rear tread width, and a front end that could be driven between crop rows—allowed the CC to be used in the plowing, cultivating, and harvesting operations of any type crop.

The CC was fitted with independent differential foot brakes that shortened the tractor's turning radius and made faster turns possible. The CC was available with a number of options including power take-off (PTO), rubber tires, rear wheel extensions, and electric starter and lights. In 1935, Case introduced Motor-Lift, a mechanical power lift for raising and lowering implements, which increased the speed and efficiency of operations.

Besides standard and row-crop configurations, the C was also offered as the industrial Model CI, orchard Model CO, vineyard Model CO-VS, sugar cane Model CCS, and high-clearance Model CH. The Model CC was fitted with either a narrow front as the Model CC-3 or standard front as the CC-4.

Model RC and R of 1935–1940

In 1932, International Harvester introduced the Farmall F-12, a 14-hp, one-to-two-plow general-purpose tractor. In an era when 60 percent of America's farms were smaller than 100 acres (40 hectares), such a tractor made sense—a general-purpose tractor at a price the average farmer could afford. Case too saw the potential in this small tractor market, and in 1935, introduced the Model RC.

Although the RC did not resemble the CC, it offered similar features. The RC was powered by a four-cylinder Waukesha Model FK engine cast *en bloc* with renewable cylinder sleeves and a three-speed transmission. It had roller-chain final drive, an adjustable rear axle, independent differential brakes, a PTO as standard equipment, a choice of single or dual front wheels and a choice of steel wheels or rubber tires.

A number of modifications were made to the RC during the course of production. Introduced with an overhead steering shaft and extended steering post, the system was changed to that used on the CC in 1937. In 1938, Case offered an optional adjustable front axle. In 1939, a four-speed transmission, Motor-Lift, and optional electrics were introduced. The RC was also restyled in 1939 with a more streamlined and rounder grille and hood treatment. The color of the RC was also changed, from the gray used on all Case tractors in the 1930s, to Flambeau Red, the color of the newest series of Case tractors introduced in 1939.

In 1938, Case introduced a standard version of the RC, the Model R. It featured the same engine and transmission fitted to the RC. Fenders were standard, but PTO was optional. Case offered the R as both industrial and orchard tractors. In 1939, it was updated in the same manner as the RC.

Model R, 1939
The Model R was introduced as a standard version of the row-crop RC in 1938. Re-styled in 1939, it introduced the Case concept of "Eagle-Eye Visibility." According to Case, "the new tractors provided enhanced visibility, a better clutch mechanism, lower friction gearshift levers, and more efficient, positive pressure oiling systems. A fourth gear was added to the stronger, smoother power-saving transmission, and a time-saving electric starter."

Case Catalog With Model L, circa 1930

The new Model L and its smaller companion, the Model C, were radically different from the Crossmotors that they replaced. The engine was no longer transversely mounted, and the unitized construction eliminated the need for a distinct frame. The Models L and C also introduced chain-driven final drives, a feature Case employed for the next three decades. (Photo courtesy Shields Library, Special Collections, University of California, Davis)

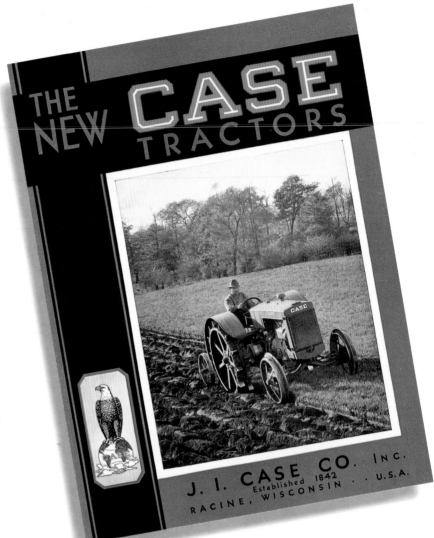

Model L Plowing, 1929

The Case Model L tractor was introduced in 1929 after four years of extensive testing and field trials. The new design furnished power in three useful ways: via drawbar, belt, and power take-off. It was especially favored by farmers because of easy access to all parts for service and repairs. Here, a Model L pulls a 10-foot (300-cm) double disk fluted feed drill in tandem behind a 10-foot (300-cm) WL Series Wheatland Plow.

THE NEW CASE TRACTORS

Model "L"
Above is the New Case Model "L" Tractor. This is the 3-4 plow size (depending on soil conditions) adaptable to a wide range of drawbar, belt and power take-off work. It weighs only a little more than 3 draft horses.

Model "C"
Here is the new Case Model "C" Tractor. Although it weighs but little more than 2 draft horses, it handles a 2 or 3 bottom 14-inch plow (depending on soil conditions) and other loads of similar power requirements.

Page Twenty-four

ABOVE: Model L, 1938
Case offered a long list of options and accessories for its tractors, including this factory-built cab, fitted here to a Model L.

LEFT: Models L and C, 1931
Case's 1931 catalog offered the Models L and C, as well as the row-crop CC, and the industrial CI.

You can now get in the new Case Model "L" tractor advantages you have long desired—advantages which will enable you to do your work better, faster and at less cost.
—Case Model L brochure, 1930s

RIGHT: Case Russian Catalog, 1931
Case had a long history of sales to Russia. In 1931, with the introduction of the Models L and C, Case prepared this Russian-language catalog.

BELOW: Model L Cutaway, circa 1930
Case lauded its new generation of tractors as "The New Case Tractor . . . Years Ahead." This cutaway of the Model L details the engineering advances Case had made over the old Crossmotors.

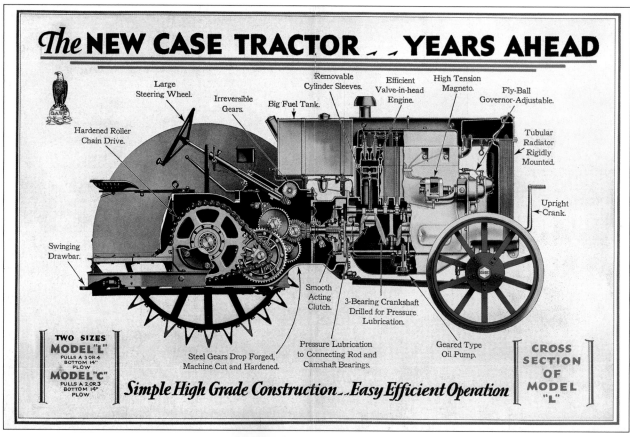

ABOVE, LEFT: Case Catalog, circa 1930
Case promised forty ways that power farming would pay in this booklet.

ABOVE, RIGHT: Case Postcard, circa 1930s

BELOW: Model L at Work, 1930
The Model L was a standard tractor with fixed front- and rear-axle tread widths. It ably handled a variety of drawbar tasks. Here, a Model L pulls a Case Model P combine fitted with windrower and pickup attachment.

ABOVE: Model C Harvesting Corn, 1934
The Model C standard tractor, shown pulling a Model R-3TP power corn binder, offered all the features of the Model L but was built on a smaller scale.

RIGHT: Model C, 1931
The Model C was a compact version of the big Model L.

FOR PROFITABLE FARMING

Left Side of Model "C" Showing Compact Construction.

Four Big Advantages

AMONG the numerous features of the new Case tractors, four big advantages are outstanding.

Adaptable to Your Needs

Their performance on soft land, wet soil, sand, clay, rocky land; on level fields, hilly fields or side slopes is unusually satisfactory. They will work efficiently in any climate and all seasons. They have abundant power for heavy work within their power range, and are highly efficient on the lighter jobs.

Power is delivered to drawbar, belt or power take-off. Three forward speeds offer a range suitable for every kind of drawbar work.

Dependable and Durable

Long, severe field trials, confirmed by thousands of users, have proven that the new Case tractors offer you something unusual in dependability and durability. They are strongly made of high quality tested materials and are manufactured under expert supervision. The entire tractor is sealed against dirt and most parts automatically lubricated.

Ease of Handling

A boy can handle the new Case as easily as a full grown man. Later, on page 15, you will

see the care with which all controls are placed for ease of operation. The whole machine is extremely simple to care for and to operate.

Economy of Operation

The new Case sets a new high mark for fuel economy on maximum loads, on rated loads and on varying loads.

The durability and accessibility of these tractors makes them easy and inexpensive to keep in good working order throughout many long years of service.

The Model "C" Pulls a 2 or 3 Bottom Plow.

Page Five

ABOVE: Models L and C Flyer, circa 1930s
This flyer promised that "There's a New Case Trac-
tor For Every Need."

LEFT: Model CC Catalog
The horizons were broad with the new Case Model
CC general-purpose tractor.

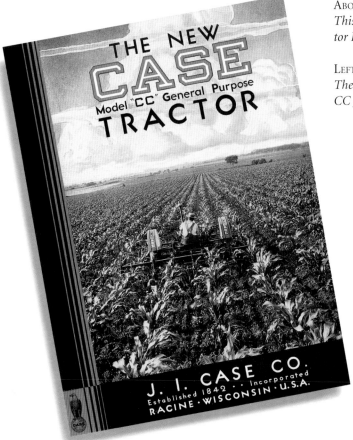

RIGHT, TOP: Model CC-3 Driving
Thresher, 1932
The Model CC-3 provided auxiliary power via its standard belt pulley or optional power take-off. This CC-3 operated an 1880s vintage Case 32x54 agitator thresher to thresh oats on the farm of John Weber in South Milwaukee

RIGHT, BOTTOM: Model CC with
Combine, 1937
The Case Model CC was the first Case tractor that successfully combined the advantages of a plowing and a cultivating tractor into one unit. Introduced in 1931, the Model CC offered adjustable rear-wheel spacing from the standard 48-inch (120-cm) tread for plowing up to 84 inches (210 cm) for row-crop planting and cultivating. Here, a CC is equipped with Firestone rubber tires, pulling a Case A–6 combine that is cutting and picking oats that had gone down in a wind storm.

BELOW: Model CI for Russia, 1931
The Model CI was the designation for the industrial version of the Model C, offered here in the Case Russian catalog of 1931.

35777

TRACTOR AND IMPLEMENTS

1. The "CC" with Wheels Set in to Standard Tractor Tread—a first class Plowing Tractor

2. The "CC" with Wheels Set out—a Highly Efficient Planting and Cultivating Tractor

The New Case Model "CC"—
2 Tractors in One for All Purposes

THIS new Case tractor is really two tractors in one, adaptable to every farm power operation. It is a first class plowing type tractor easily converted into a highly efficient planting and cultivating tractor. You simply widen the tread to make the change.

1. The "CC" as a Plowing Type Tractor

As a plowing tractor the rear wheels are spaced at the standard tractor tread of 48 inches. Since tractor plows and other implements work better behind standard tread tractors, this feature eliminates side draft, hard steering and awkward hitches. In this form, as shown in illustration No. 1 above, it makes a better power

unit for such work as plowing, harrowing and harvesting. The "CC" is available as either a three or four wheel plowing type tractor.

2. The "CC" as a Planting and Cultivating Tractor

For planting and cultivating, the rear wheels are easily set out to fit the rows, as shown in illustration 2 above. A special feature of the Case is the wide variety of rear wheel treads possible, as illustrated on page 5. The rear wheels can be spaced at various treads to accommodate most any width of rows.

No other tractor has such a wide range of adaptability as the New Case Model "CC."

ABOVE: Model CC-3 General-Purpose, 1935
The Model CC-3, the first Case general-purpose tractor, was promoted as a two-to-three-plow tractor. Here, it pulls a two-bottom Case B-24 plow.

LEFT: Model CC Catalog
The Model CC, the first Case general-purpose tractor, was promoted as a two-to-three-plow tractor.

There is a Case Tractor for every farming job.
—Case Models L and C
brochure, 1930s

For **EVERY CROP AND EVERY JOB**

CASE "CC" ALL-PURPOSE TRACTOR

ABOVE: Model CC Chases Farming Gremlins, circa 1930s
Case advertised the virtues of the Model CC in this colorful manner in the mid-1930s.

LEFT: Model CC Catalog, circa 1930s

THESE FARMING HAZARDS. . .

facts

There are but two things that will help you combat bad weather, late work, killing heat, weeds and the many other handicaps . . . they are *Speed* and *Power*. The Case "CC" Tractor travels twice as fast at field work as the ordinary working gait of horses. It has three speeds so you can select the one best suited for the job you are doing.

TWICE AS FAST AS ANIMALS

It is the extra work capacity that gives you added control over all your farming operations. One owner says: "It is better than 10 horses and an extra man." It is better because you can do more work with it at a fraction of the cost. When it has done all your drawbar work, you will find it equally satisfactory for belt operations—threshing, filling silos, grinding feed, etc.

DOES THE WORK OF FOUR TEAMS

The Case "CC" weighs from ½ to nearly a ton less than other tractors of similar power rating. Think of the fuel alone that this saves—and how much more of the engine's power is available for doing useful work. The Case has just the right weight in front to make steering easy and there's ample weight over the rear wheels to give good traction. You can start work earlier in the season because with this tractor you can go through soft spots when a heavier tractor would mire down and be useless.

SAVES TIME ON THE TURNS

With the Case there is no time lost on the turns. A touch on a foot trigger causes the power lift to raise or lower the implement, making it unnecessary to stop at the ends of rows or to manipulate lifting levers. The independent differential brakes assist the operator in swinging around quickly in the shortest possible space and time. As one owner writes, "With the handy foot brakes on the "CC," anyone can turn it in the same space in which a team of horses can be turned." This quick turning enables the "CC" to cover more ground each hour.

DAY AND NIGHT IF NEED BE

Here is a new kind of power that is always ready to go. It doesn't tire nor get sore shoulders or lame muscles in spring. It is free from the dangers of killing heat, flies and other insects. If your work needs rushing, the Case "CC" can stay on the job 24 hours a day.

3 •

Case Logo
(Photograph © by Dave Arnold

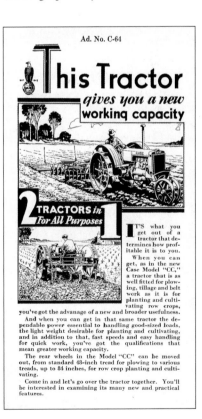

Model CC Ad, circa 1930s
Case promised that the row-crop CC would deliver "2 Tractors in 1 For All Purposes."

There are but two things that will help you combat bad weather, late work, killing heat, weeds and the many other handicaps . . . they are Speed *and* Power.
—Case Model CC brochure, 1930s

For Every Crop and Every Job.
—Case Model CC brochure,
1930s

FACING PAGE, TOP: Model CD Crawler Flyer, circa 1930s
A track-equipped Model CI, referred to as a CD Trackson. Aftermarket tracklaying equipment for the CI was available from a number of manufacturers.

FACING PAGE, BOTTOM: Model CI Industrial, circa 1930s
Model CI was the designation for the industrial version of the Model C. Pictured here is a CI golf course special.

BELOW: Model CD Crawler, 1930

Above: Model R
A restored Model R Standard. (Photograph © by Dave Arnold)

Facing page, top: Model RC Catalog, 1936
The Model RC, introduced in 1936, was marketed to the small farmer for "doing all the farm work with amazing economy" and to large farms for "doing light jobs the cheapest way known." Its principal competition was the International Harvester Farmall F-12.

Facing page, bottom: Models RC and R Catalog, 1939
The RC was restyled in 1939, with rounder lines and a new grille. Steering had changed from the overhead system to the "chicken-roost" side-steer system of the CC in 1937.

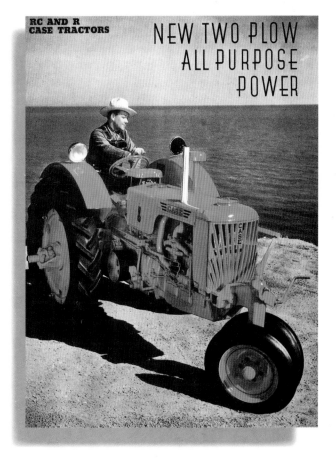

RIGHT: Model CCS, circa 1930s
Case also offered the Model C as a high-clearance cane tractor, the Model CCS.

BELOW, RIGHT: Model CO Ad, circa 1930s
The Model CO orchard tractor featured full fenders and covered front wheels to protect orchard trees from getting caught in the tractor.

BELOW, LEFT: Model CO, circa 1930
Case offered the Model C as the CO "Orchard Special" equipped with fully enclosed fenders.

The Case "CCS" Cane Tractor

New EQUIPMENT You Have Been Wanting!

Ad. No. C-79

The day has come

—for an Orchard Tractor
that really fits the Job

IF ever a tractor fitted the purpose for which it was intended, it is this new Model "CO" Case Tractor. Here is a machine that is made to the last detail for efficient work in fruit groves, vineyards and orchards.

You will be amazed at the compactness of this tractor. It is built low and light . . . stands only 48 inches high . . . weighs but little more than two draft horses . . . has dependable power for drawbar, belt and power take-off work.

The rear wheels are well enclosed by new sloping fenders which lift low hanging branches and permit the tractor to travel close to trees . . . the front wheels are of the solid disk type. Short turning under full loads, easy maneuvering, fast speeds, and handy controls, are other important advantages.

Never before has a tractor like it been offered to you. Its absolute fitness for your particular kind of work will enable you to speed up every operation and make more money. Come in and see it. We can also show you many other new Case machines.

(DEALER'S NAME, ADDRESS AND PHONE NUMBER TO BE SET HERE)

CASE
FULL LINE OF CASE QUALITY FARM MACHINES

FOR PROFITABLE FARMING

ORCHARD SPECIAL

CASE

The Model "CO" is Low, Compact, Powerful and Short Turning with Full Load.

The New Case Orchard Tractor Model "CO"

REALIZING that orchard and grove work requires a tractor different from ordinary farm tractors, Case engineers developed the new Case orchard tractor right in the orchards and groves of California.

The field studies were made in places where these machines are used. A great many experimental tractors were tested and tried out in the worst field conditions that could be found.

As a result, the new Case Model "CO" tractor perfected under these conditions, offers many superior advantages for orchard, grove and vineyard work.

Low and Compact
It is low, short and narrow. All parts are covered so there are no projections to catch on limbs. It steers easily and turns inside a 10 foot radius. Moreover it pulls big loads on the turns as well as on the straight pulls.

Independent foot brakes acting on the differential are a great help when many short turns must be made in loose soil.

Specially Equipped
You will notice by the above illustration that it has high 3 inch skid rings for easier steering and high sand lugs for good traction in light soils. The disk wheels shown are extra equipment at slight additional cost. Note that the full orchard fenders cover the wheels and have an easy forward slope for lifting low branches without damage.

The Model "L" for Orchards
Where more power is required than that available in the Model "CO", the Model "L" provides an ideal orchard tractor. It can often be used as regularly equipped for any other farm work, but can also be equipped with full enclosing fenders, high sand lugs and 3 inch skid rings.

Further information is given in a special folder on the new Case Orchard tractors. A copy will be gladly sent on request.

Pulls Full Loads on Short Turns.

360024

LEFT: Model RC, 1936
At introduction, the RC featured a Waukesha four-cylinder engine, three-speed transmission, and overhead steering. Rubber tires were optional.

BELOW: Model R
This 1938 Model R is owned by Otto Reynolds of Rock Creek, Minnesota.
(Photograph © by Dave Arnold)

ABOVE: Model RC
As with the other Case tractors, the old Model RC was updated with a Flambeau Red paint scheme. This restored example was shown at the 1989 Rough and Tumble Thrashers Show in Kinzers, Pennsylvania. (Photograph © by Dave Arnold)

FACING PAGE, TOP: Model RI, 1938
The industrial tractor Model RI and an orchard tractor Model RO were both limited-production units based on the Model R. The RI featured standard four-speed transmission, electric starter and lights, industrial seat, and a foot accelerator.

FACING PAGE, BOTTOM: Model RC
A restored 1936 Model RC. (Photograph © by Dave Arnold)

83

"What Mother Thinks of Case Machinery"

It was a fact of life that most farm tractors and implements were sold to men in the first half of this century, but Case was clever in using the farm wife's testimonial to help sells its products, as this selection from an early brochure shows:

Poets and artists have for years painted with brush and word, the beauty and joy of the harvest. It may have had certain elements of pleasure for the men—but not for the mother of the farm home. To her it was anything but a happy, gay or festive time. On the contrary it was a time of her hardest work and greatest mental and nervous strain. Mother was virtually a slave, in every sense of the word, to the cook-stove, the dish-pan and the wash-tub during the heat of the summer's hottest days.

Now, however, all of this has been changed, for the miracle machine of modern agriculture—the combine—has struck off the shackles which for years have bound mother to days and weeks of drudgery during the harvest time. The combine has completely revolutionized modern harvest operations and has truly emancipated mother from the back-breaking and nerve-straining drudgery of the harvest season.

No longer is "Mother" a galley slave to his majesty, the cook-stove, or his highness, the dish-pan, or the tyrant, the wash-tub during the blazing hot days of mid-summer. No longer is her beloved and cherished home a bunk-house for a hungry horde of harvest hands, many times undesirable characters recruited from the slums of the great cities. This has all been changed—for now "father and the boys can do it all."

Since the advent of a Case combine, mother has learned what a great pleasure harvest can really be. She has likewise discovered how many pleasures and conveniences of a modern home can be secured with the many savings made possible by a Case combine.

Wishing to learn first-hand just exactly what mother thought of the Case combine, we wrote to a group of combine owners asking the women to write to us in their own way. Many letters expressing heart-felt gratitude were received from all parts of the country. Here are a small number received from happy mothers. We give them to you, not as our words, but as the statements of "What Mother Thinks of the Case Combine."

"The country women who have gone through the drudgery of harvest without a combine can fully appreciate the real labor-saving device we have in the combine."
—Mrs. E. H. Grimes, White Deer, Texas

"No worry to cook for the men."
—Mrs. J. D. Faulkenberg, Carmen, Okla.

"Will relieve the problem of cooking for threshers."
—Mrs. Ernest Painter, La Harpe, Ill.

"I enjoyed my harvest as never before."
—Mrs. Harry N. Husted, Kinsley, Kansas

"I appreciate very much the fact that so few men are required."
—Mrs. Homer Wilson, Ferdinand, Idaho

"Had time to do a lot of canning."
—Mrs. A. G. Ballensky, Rock Springs, Mont.

"Gentlemen:

My husband has been a wheat grower for eighteen years. During this time I have cooked for a great number of men. It was impossible to get help unless a neighbor would come and assist at the noon meal. Most of the time this was impossible as each of us had more than we should have done at home.

During the harvests gathered with binders or headers, I had to cook for from fifteen to twenty-two men. Quantities of food had to be prepared, and I am sure it never did get hotter in the harvest field than it was over the kitchen range, the top of which was covered with pots of boiling vegetables and frying meats, while the oven was filled with pies, buns and bread.

From four in the morning until ten at night it was almost a constant round of cooking, baking and washing dishes. The pleasant experience of the entire weary drag of work was when the last man left and the family was alone once more.

Those who perfected the combine have given the farm world one of the greatest labor-saving devices. This year we harvested nine hundred acres of wheat, and I had but three extra men. The entire crop was harvested with two Case combines and all the work easily completed within three weeks."
—Mrs. E. H. Grimes

These happy enthusiastic letters could only have been written by women who were thankful for the many blessings they have received as a result of the combine on their place. But these are not all of the advantages of the combine by any means—there are many, many more. These have indirect influence upon "Mother." They make possible the ultimate financial success of the whole farm, thus giving "Mother" additional funds with which to purchase those improvements, luxuries and conveniences which make for a peaceful and happy home life in general.

Long, severe field tests were made under the most varied and difficult conditions that could be found, from the sticky gumbo soil of Texas to the dusty orchards of California. Whenever an unusually tough job was heard of, these Case tractors were sent there to do it.
—"The New Case Tractors" brochure, 1930s

Chapter 6

Zenith of the General Purpose Tractors

The Flambeau Red Era, 1939–1955

The tractor business is coming of age. There are brighter days ahead for dealers who offer better tractors, better value, better fit of tractor to farm. It's time to consider seriously the Case contract, your surest way to substantial success.
—Case catalog, 1950s

LEFT: Model SC
1948 Case SC owned by Bruce Nelson of St. Croix Falls, Wisconsin. (Photograph © by Dave Arnold)

ABOVE: Case Catalog With D Series, 1939
The D Series tractors were introduced with great fanfare in 1939. The first new tractors of the Flambeau Red series, the standard D and row-crop DC offered "50 modern conveniences," according to the company.

Case continued to upgrade and refine its general-purpose tractors in the 1940s and 1950s. Competition from Ford, International Harvester, and Deere was intense, so Case could not rest on its laurels. Existing model lines were revised, restyled, and repainted in the now-famous Flambeau Red that has come to signify the zenith of Case's general-purpose tractors in the classic years.

New Replaces the Old: D Series of 1939–1953

The influence of industrial designers reached new heights in the 1930s, as manufacturers of everything from toasters to skyscrapers sought a more modern, streamlined look. Tractor manufacturers were no exception, as rectangular lines gave way to smoother, rounder shapes. The Model C and Model CC were representative of the old school of design, with prominent cast-iron radiators, simple rectangular hoods, and squared-off fenders. When Case restyled the C Series and planned the change of paint scheme from gray to Flambeau Red, the decision was made to redesignate the model line as the D Series.

Other than styling, little else distinguished the new series. The first five hundred units were fitted with the three-speed transmission from the C Series. Subsequent units carried a four-speed transmission, with a top speed of 9 to 10 mph (14–16 km/h). The engine was virtually unchanged. A new four-ring piston replaced the three-ring piston of the C Series, but displacement was not increased. The DC was available with a choice of "many-fuel" or "economy gasoline" manifolds.

The D Series included the standard Model D, rated as a three-plow tractor; row-crop models DC-3, DH, and DC-4; orchard and vineyard models DO and DV; industrial models DI Standard and DI Narrow; and a sugar cane–special DCS. Special export and military tractors were also built.

Over the course of production, the D Series tractors were modified and updated to maintain their competitive edge. The introduction of hydraulic lift, high-compression, and LPG options, live hydraulics and PTO, and the addition of Eagle Hitch were among the most significant changes. By 1955, when the 400 Series replaced the D, Case had built more than 100,000 D Series tractors.

The Little Tractor That Could: V Series of 1940–1942

The acceptance of the R Series confirmed the demand for smaller gen-

Model DC-3, 1945
The 1945 DC-3 featured optional electrics.

eral-purpose and standard tractors. The Case V Series, which replaced the R Series, was manufactured using key components bought from outside suppliers. The four-cylinder engine was built by Continental Motors of Muskegon, Michigan. Although Case cast the transmission and final-drive housings, the gearing was supplied by Clark Company of Michigan.

The V Series was produced in four configurations: standard Model V; row-crop Model VC; industrial Model VI; and orchard Model VO. Rated as a one-to-two-plow tractor, the V Series offered a four-speed transmission, all-gear final drive, and a range of standard and optional features that included PTO, electric starter and lights, adjustable front axle, and both narrow and wide rear tread options.

Although produced for only three years, more than 15,000 V Series tractors were built before Case introduced the venerable Model VA.

Model LA of 1940–1952

The Model L proved to be a popular tractor, although sales were somewhat depressed due to the economic conditions of the early to mid-1930s. In August 1940, its successor the LA was introduced. The LA was built as a standard, rice-special, industrial, and military tractor.

The LA received new sheet metal, with a rounded grille, hood, and fenders, and a Flambeau Red paint job. Mechanically, little other than a higher-compression cylinder head differentiated the new model. Soon after introduction, the four-speed transmission fitted to the LI replaced the three-speed unit carried over from the L. The LA options included PTO, electric starter and lights, and hydraulics.

In 1942, Case built the first of the LA and LAI models equipped with the Hesselman fuel-injection system. The system, which effectively allowed a standard Case spark-ignited engine to burn diesel fuel, had been available for the L in limited quantities. Developed in Sweden and licensed to Waukesha Engine, the technology offered distinct advantages over a conventional diesel engine, chief among them being the ease with which the engine could be started compared to a high-compression diesel engine. The Hesselman engine could also burn almost any grade of fuel. The Hesselman engine was not a true diesel engine, however, and did not offer the same performance characteristics or economies of engine life and fuel economy as did a diesel. It, therefore, was not as successful as future Case diesels.

In 1952, Case introduced LPG equipment for the LA. Although more economical than gasoline in some parts of the country, LPG options were also of limited success.

Case Dealer Sign, circa 1950s

S Series of 1941–1954

The S Series filled the void in horsepower between the V and D Series, and put Case in a more competitive position. The S resembled the D, and in many ways was simply a smaller version. The designs of its steering, transmission, and final drives were similar.

The S engine, however, was a short-stroke, high-rpm design that maximized horsepower output from the smaller and lighter engine. Offered with both gas and low-cost fuel options, the 3½x4-inch (87.5x100-mm)

PROVED POWER
for Faster Farming

MODEL "D" SERIES
CASE
TRACTORS • 3-PLOW SIZE

ABOVE: Model D at Work, 1939
Improved visibility was first on the list of fifty modern conveniences. A raised platform on the standard D elevated the operator and allowed a direct line of vision to the front wheel and down the furrow.

LEFT: Model DC-3, 1939
The DC-3, available with dual or single front wheel, was the most popular configuration of D Series tractors. This 1939 model was fitted with optional rubber tires.

FACING PAGE, INSET: Case Catalog With D Series, circa 1940s
Case's catalogs were full of stylish graphics promoting its tractor models. This 1940s D Series catalog used the tractor's running lamps to highlight the D Series notation. Old Abe shown above like a full moon.

*Here is power enough to double the work
one man can do in a day with ordinary tractors.*
—Case Model LA brochure, 1940s

RIGHT, TOP: Model DC, 1952
The 1949 DC introduced Hydraulic Control in place of Motor-Lift. An optional portable hydraulic cylinder allowed remote control of pull-type implements. The 1952 DC brought live hydraulics and PTO as well as the addition of Eagle Hitch, Case's answer to Harry Ferguson's three-point-hitch design.

RIGHT, BOTTOM: Model DC-3, 1953
As featured on this 1953 DC-3, an optional adjustable front axle was offered the final two years of production. This particular unit was fitted with an experimental diesel engine.

BELOW: Model DI, 1939
The 1939 industrial Model DI Standard Tread offered a tread width of 60 inches (150 cm), expandable to 94 inches (235 cm) with dual wheels. A narrow version designed to work in tight areas, the DI Narrow Tread, measured 48 inches (120 cm) outside width. Unlike the hand-operated clutch of the D and DC, both industrial models featured a foot-operated clutch.

New Case Model "DI" Industrial Tractor

Model "DI" tractor equipped with low pressure tires, lights and fenders available at extra cost.

New Performance, Speed, Flexibility and Comfort

The new Case Model "DI" tractor retains all the time-proven advantages of previous Case Industrial Tractors and has numerous new features.

Model "DI" tractor with low pressure tires. Note vertical adjustable drawbar and upholstered industrial seat as well as convenient operating controls and instrument panel.

New Advantages mean New Endurance

The heavy-duty, four-cylinder engine has increased power with greater flexibility over the entire speed range. An improved lubrication system assures full pressure oiling to main, connecting rod and camshaft bearings, valves in the rocker arms and governor parts. Drilled passages in the engine block eliminate all inside oil pipes. Pressure lubrication is also provided to the clutch pilot bearing and all clutch operating parts.

Refinements in the cooling and carburetion systems assure greater fuel and oil economy under all operating conditions. The radiator is provided with an adjustable shutter and protected by a sturdy guard.

Four Forward Gears

The power saving transmission of Case tractors is retained in the Model "DI" with four forward gears and one reverse, giving a greater range of travel speeds. Improved oil seals, permanent inside rear axle bearing and stronger, improved gears throughout add to the life of the transmission.

Convenient Operation

Operators will find the Model "DI" easy and convenient to handle. Easier steering results because the steering gear ratio has been increased. Auto-type gear shift lever permits easier gear shifting. An instrument panel groups instruments and controls right under the operator's eyes. The sponge rubber upholstered, spring mounted industrial seat with backrest, with foot clutch and brakes have been retained. A platform, composition steering wheel, as well as roomy operating controls.

Streamlined improved and refined, the Case Model "DI" will give years of dependable, economical operation.

Write for more complete information.

Model VC, 1940
The row-crop VC was the most popular of the four configurations of the short-lived V Series. This early production model powers a Case A-6 combine.

gas unit produced a maximum 21.62 brake hp at 1,550 rpm. Toward the end of its production run, bore was increased to 3⅜ inches (84 mm), and in its official Nebraska test, the new engine produced a maximum 29.68 brake hp.

The S Series was available in the standard Model S; row-crop Model SC; grove and orchard Model SO; and industrial Model SI. A popular series for Case, the company sold nearly 84,000 units before the S was succeeded by the 300 Series in 1955.

The Venerable GP Tractor: VA Series of 1942–1955

Easily the best-selling series of collectible Case tractors, the VA Series succeeded the V Series in 1942. The market for one-plow tractors was keen. The V had faced stiff price competition from the Farmall A and Allis-Chalmers B. By bringing production of a new Case engine (initially assembled by Continental) and gearing in-house, Case gained tighter control over both supply and costs.

Although the V and VA resembled each other, the two had almost no parts in common. The VA four-cylinder engine featured an overhead camshaft and 3¼x3¾-inch (81x93.75-mm) bore and stroke. Early units operated on gasoline only. In 1947, Case introduced the Low Cost Fuel manifold. The VA four-speed transmission and all-gear final drive were newly designed.

The VA Series was built in a broad range of tractors: the standard Model VA; dual-wheel tricycle Model VAC and VAC-12 (produced 1951–1953); single-front-wheel row-crop VAC-11; adjustable wide-front row-crop Model VAC-13; adjustable wide-front, low-profile row-crop Model VAC-14; industrial Model VAI; orchard Model VAO; low-profile orchard Model VAO-15; warehouse and towmotor tractor Model VAIW; high-clearance row-crop Model VAH; and the offset high-clearance row-crop Model VAS.

Over 66 Different Farm Jobs Made Easier.
—Case S Series brochure, 1940s

RIGHT: Case Logo
(Photograph © by Dave Arnold)

BELOW: Case Catalog with D, 1952
In 1952, Case introduced optional LPG equipment for the D and the larger LA Series tractors. Conversion kits were offered for older D Series tractors.

Dust-Proof Throughout.
—Case D Series brochure, 1940s

A FULL LINE OF TRACTORS

MODEL "DC"
3-PLOW

A leader among larger all-purpose tractors. The Case "DC" provides full three-plow power to hustle the heavy work and keep ahead of weeds and weather. Rear wheel spacings from 48 to 84 inches—96 inches with special rear axle. Available with single front wheel or adjustable front axle for narrow-row cultivation. Free catalog describes all "D" models.

MODEL "SC"
FULL 2-PLOW

Here is full Case quality and performance in a tractor with plenty of capacity for all 2-plow farming. "S" series tractors are fast-working, dependable, convenient. "SC" rear wheels may be spaced from 44 to 80 inches — 96 inches with special rear axle. Also available with single front wheel or adjustable front axle. Free catalog gives full details.

MODEL "VAC"
LIGHT 2-PLOW

Full 2-row capacity, complete equipment, and Case endurance — all in a low-cost tractor. Handles 2 plows in many soils, one-bottom under tough conditions. Rear wheels adjust from 44 to 80 inches in tread width — 88-inch with special axles. Available with adjustable front axle or single front wheel, if desired. Tractor and implements described in free catalog.

J. I. CASE CO. INC., RACINE, WISCONSIN, U.S.A.

Serving Agriculture Since 1842

Form A765   Printed in U. S. A.

ABOVE: Model DC
The Model DC featured a four-cylinder engine of 3⅞x5½-inch (97x137.5-mm) bore and stroke. The engine produced 25 drawbar hp and 32 brake hp. The price of the DC-3 was $1,040 on steel wheels and $1,270 on rubber in 1944, and $2,465 on rubber in 1952. This restored DC is owned by Tim Reynolds of Rock Creek, Minnesota. (Photograph © by Dave Arnold)

LEFT: Case Lineup, circa 1940s
By the 1940s, Case offered a full array of general-purpose tractors to combat the International Harvester Farmall's market dominance. The line included the light-duty two-plow VAC, heavy-duty two-plow SC, and the three-plow DC.

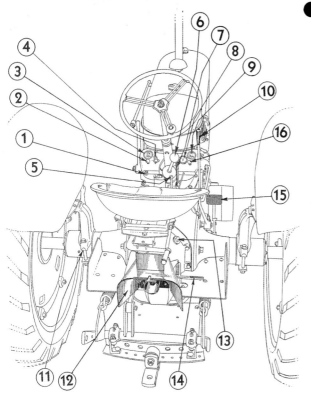

Fig. 2. Controls and Instruments

1. Choke
2. Magneto Grounding Switch
3. Temperature Gauge
4. Starter Switch
5. Throttle Lever
6. Gear Shift Lever
7. Power Take-Off Shifter
8. Ammeter Gauge
9. Oil Pressure Gauge
10. Clutch Lever
11. Adjustable Fender Bracket
12. Master Shield
13. Transmission Filler Plug
14. Power Lift Pedal
15. Brake Pedal, R. H.
16. Light Switch

8

LEFT, TOP: S Series Controls, 1943
The Operator's Instruction Book detailed the controls and instruments on the S and SC models.

LEFT, BOTTOM: Model SC, 1941
The SC and the standard S were fitted with a short-stroke, high-rpm four-cylinder engine that produced nearly 22 hp.

5 great models FOR EVERY JOB IN ANY FARMING SYSTEM · · ·

Case "S" series tractors are made in five different models to meet every farming need for modern, proved power with full two-plow capacity. The three basic tractors are the "SC," an all-purpose tractor for cultivating as well as general farm work; the "S" with standard 4-wheel design; and the "SO" for orchard and grove work. In addition to these,

the "SC" tractor is available in models with a single front wheel and with an extensible front axle which allows the front wheel treads to fit any row spacing. Special "SC" rear axles also permit rear wheel tread widths up to 96 inches. Regular front-mounted cultivators and other implements can be used with all three tractors of the "SC" type.

ON MOST FARMS

The all-purpose "SC" with twin front wheels provides ideal power for every job on most diversified farms. Key and groove rear axles provide any tread width from 44 to 80 inches. Pivot turning is aided by efficient disk-type assisting brakes. Mounted tools are raised and lowered by versatile hydraulic control.

66 JOBS

DRAWBAR WORK
Plowing
Disking
Harrowing
Leveling
Subsoiling
Pulverizing
Cultivating or "Duckfooting"
Seeding
Listing or Planting
Raking Hay
Sweep Raking
Loading Hay
Stacking Hay
Hoisting Hay
Binding
Windrowing
Combining
Cutting Corn
Spreading Manure or Lime
Grading
Excavating
Pulling Stumps
Building Fences

Terracing
Pond Building
Hauling
Filling Ditches
Spraying
Laying Tile
Cutting Stalks

BELT WORK
Threshing
Hulling Clover
Picking Peanuts
Silo Filling
Feed Grinding
Hay Chopping
Stationary Baling
Sawing Wood
Shelling Corn
Shelling Green Peas
Pumping Water
Drying Hay
Drying Grain
Cleaning Grain
Machine Milking

Elevating Grain
Crushing Rock
Powdering Lime

POWER TAKE-OFF WORK
Picking Corn
Binding
Field Chopping
Baling
Pick-up Baling
Combining
Mowing
Spraying
Dusting

ROW-CROP WORK (SC)
Planting
Listing
Narrow-Row Planting
Middlebusting
Rotary Hoeing
Cultivating
Narrow-Row Cultivating
Beet Pulling
Cutting Corn or Stalks

For Narrow Rows, the special Model "SC" tractor with single front wheel provides fast, efficient cultivation. Extra-long rear axles are also available to fit "SC" tractors for unusual row spacings requiring extra rear tread widths.

Extensible Front Axle equips this special Model "SC" tractor for truck-crop requirements or for steep hillside farming. Front wheels are adjustable to line up with rear wheel tread from 56 to 80 inches in width.

The Standard Model "S" tractor brings modern two-plow power to farms where row-crop cultivation is not a factor. The Model "S" is short-turning and easily handled. Equipped with pulley; power take-off is available.

For Grove Work, the Model "SO" provides two-plow power to a fully equipped orchard tractor with disk-type turning brakes and well-shielded to protect valuable tree limbs and fruit. Power take-off is available for sprayer operation.

ABOVE: Model SC Catalog, 1941
The row-crop SC was positioned between the smaller VC, and its successor VAC, and the larger DC. Early units are distinguished by intake and exhaust pipes that pass through the hood, flat rear wheels, and deep shell fenders.

FACING PAGE, TOP: Model S Standard
The engine for the Model S was a four-cylinder of 3½x4-inch (87.5x100-mm) bore and stroke. The engine created 16.18 drawbar hp and 21.62 brake hp. The price of the S was $845 on steel wheels and $990 on rubber in 1944. This 1945 Model S Standard is owned by Tony Reynolds of Rock Creek, Minnesota. (Photograph © by Dave Arnold)

FACING PAGE, INSET: S Series Catalog, circa 1940s
The S Series lineup included the standard S, orchard Model SO, and the general-purpose row-crop SC with either dual narrow front wheels, single narrow front, or extendable wide front axle.

ABOVE: Model LA, circa 1950s
Although production of the LA peaked in 1949, sales remained strong into 1953. A genuine five-plow tractor, its gasoline engine produced nearly 53 hp.

RIGHT: Case Poster with Model LA, circa 1940
An early poster displaying the new Model LA with the chrome strip on the side of the hood.

A Might Tractor For Heavy Work.
—Case Model LA brochure, 1940s

Another New Case Tractor
— THE MODEL "LA"

MORE TRACTOR THAN YOU EVER SAW BEFORE

IN THE **HEAVY DUTY** CLASS

You'll get a thrill out of handling this husky—it's modern in every way—with new styling, color, comfort and conveniences that make tough going and heavy duty work come easy.

But what's more important to you is its greater economy and durability—gets more power from less fuel—of whatever kind of fuel you choose—gets more work done in a day with its big power capacity and 4-speed transmission—and lasts longer because of its durable construction and improved dust sealing.

Former Case Model "L" tractors have worked for over 30 thousand hours—equivalent to more than 30 years of normal tractor use. This new "LA" is built to do more work and better work in less time, over a longer period of time—at less cost!

See your Case dealer now—find out more about this new heavy duty Case tractor—drive it—see for yourself what it will do for you in lowering your power and production costs and increasing your returns.

17 NEW CONVENIENCES

ABOVE: Model LA, 1940
An early version of the standard Model LA, distinguished by the chrome strip on the side of the hood, which was dropped during World War II. Successor to the Model L, it offered a new four-speed transmission and higher-compression cylinder head.

LEFT: Case Catalog with Model LA, circa 1940
An early catalog debuting the new Model LA. This early version of the standard Model LA featured the chrome strip on the side of the hood.

NEW CASE "LA"
HEAVY DUTY
TRACTOR

CASE

for the
BIG
POWER
JOBS

ABOVE: Models SC and DC Catalog, circa 1950s
Case launched its new Eagle Hitch system available on the full range of S and D Series. In addition to the general-purpose SC and DC shown here, the standard S and D and orchard SO and DO tractors were also available.

BELOW: Model SC-3 With Combine, 1941
The SC ably handled the tasks of plowing, planting, cultivating, grinding, and harvesting. This 1941 SC-3 pulls a Case Model A combine.

Model SC
The Model SC engine was a four-cylinder of 3½x4-inch (87.5x100-mm) bore and stroke like that of the S. But the SC fathered 22.41 drawbar hp and 29.68 brake hp. The SC cost $1,990 in 1952. This Model SC is owned by Tim Reynolds of Rock Creek, Minnesota. (Photograph © by Dave Arnold)

An Entirely New Experience in Tractor Operation.
—Case S Series brochure, 1940s

CASE "VAH"

High Clearance
Tractor and Implements

. . . with Hydraulic Control and "EAGLE HITCH"

ABOVE: Model VAH Catalog, circa 1940s
There was a VA tractor to meet every demand. The VAH, a high-clearance tractor with adjustable front axle, was used for tall, bushy, and bedded crops.

FACING PAGE, TOP: Model VA
The standard Model VA handled one to two plow bottoms. A belt pulley, as on this tractor, was an option.

FACING PAGE, INSET: VA Series Lineup, circa 1950s
The VA Series included the standard VA, general-purpose VAC with a variety of front-wheel configurations, the special high-clearance VAH, and the orchard and grove VAO.

Front-Mounted Cultivators for Clear Vision . . . Clean Work.
—Case Model VA brochure, 1940s

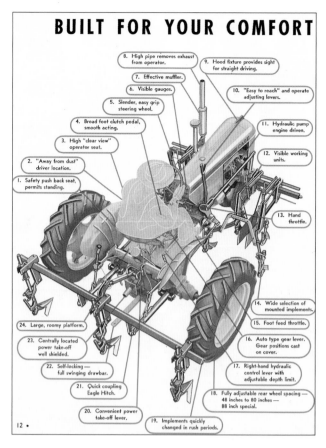

ABOVE, LEFT: Model VAC Poster, 1950
From the 1950 dealer program guide, this showroom poster was part of Case's advice on giving tractor demonstrations.

ABOVE, RIGHT: Model VAC Details, circa 1950s
Case claimed its general-purpose VAC was "Built for Comfort and Convenience at 50 Points."

RIGHT: Model VAC-13, 1952
A Model VAC-13 with adjustable front axle and Eagle Hitch pulling a Model 280 border disc plow.

Proved Power in a Smaller Package.
—Case Model VA brochure, 1940s

106

PROVED POWER
IN A SMALLER PACKAGE

CASE
"VA" SERIES TRACTORS
1-2 PLOW SIZE . . .

ABOVE: Model VAO Orchard, 1952
Although the unit depicted served as a mowing tractor, it was, in fact, a low-profile orchard Model VAO.

LEFT: VA Series Catalog, circa 1940s
Early Case catalogs for the VA Series lauded the one-to-two-plow tractor as being "Proved Power in a Smaller Package."

Case Quality

In the early part of this century, before the advent of national media and magazines, recommendations for products were often passed along by word of mouth. Thus, a satisfied Case owner was often the firm's best salesperson. And because there were many farm machinery makers in those days—some with tried-and-true ware, others with pot-boiler machines—Case always worked for quality. In prose typical of the sales pitch of the time, Case promoted the quality of its products in this early brochure selection:

It is a homely, old fashioned expression—"Big oaks from little acorns grow." The illustration below tells in a more marvelous way the story of our growth than we could explain in words. It is the growth of a small workshop started 75 years ago by Jerome I. Case to an institution which today covers 140 acres and employs over 4,000 men. In addition to the big plant there are thirty-four big branchhouses in all parts of the United States, Canada, Europe and South America.

This tremendous growth has been steady and constant. Today Case machinery is used throughout the world. Under every flag are farmers who know and respect the Case emblem. This record has been built on QUALITY PRODUCTS. That which is best is destined to endure.

The Case organization feels that with farmers it has a great mission in serving the peoples of the world. This has been our life work—to build efficiently, to build honestly and to deal fairly. Uppermost in the minds of our employees is the fact that the farmer is our customer—he must be satisfied.

For three-quarters of a century we have held steadfastly to these principles. Case quality has been handed down from generation to generation. This will always be the Case policy because time has proved that it pays farmers and pays us. You can rest assured that when you choose a Case product you buy the best that money can buy—backed by tradition, experience and thousands of friends who would have no other.

Now we start on the century mark—toward the 100 year milestone—with the agricultural outlook the greatest in the history of the world. The tremendous struggle in which so many nations are now engaged has brought forcibly to the minds of all peoples the fact that new lands must be opened, there must be more extensive cultivation—in order to supply a possible food shortage. The day of scientific farming has come. Power will soon be applied on every farm regardless of size.

In buying power farming machinery investigate and judge carefully, choose from a concern that has built its reputation on the basic principle of giving 100 cents worth for every dollar.

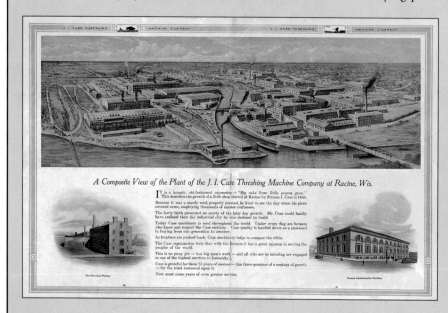

A Composite View of the Plant of the J. I. Case Threshing Machine Company at Racine, Wis.

Top: Model VAC-14, 1954
A Model VAC-14 pulls a Case Model 110 combine.

Above: Model VAC, 1942
The VA Series included the general-purpose VAC. Among collectors, it is easily the most popular Case tractor.

Bibliography

Case Steamer Plowing, circa 1910s
A Case steamer with a crew of men, women, and children plows the prairies in this Case advertising image.

Arnold, Dave. *Case Tractors: Steam to Diesel.* Osceola, WI: Motorbooks International, 1990.

Arnold, Dave. *Vintage John Deere.* Stillwater, MN: Voyageur Press, 1995.

Erb, David, and Brumbaugh, Eldon. *Full Steam Ahead: J. I. Case Tractors & Equipment 1842–1955.* St. Joseph, MI: American Society of Agricultural Engineers, 1993.

Gray, R. B. *The Agricultural Tractor: 1855–1950.* St. Joseph, MI: American Society of Agricultural Engineers, 1975.

Letourneau, Peter. *Case Tractors 1912–1959 Photo Archive.* Osceola, WI: Iconografix, 1995.

Letourneau, Peter. *Illustrated Case Tractor Buyer's Guide.* Osceola, WI: Motorbooks International, 1993.

Sanders, Ralph W. *Vintage Farm Tractors.* Stillwater, MN: Town Square Books/Voyageur Press, 1996.

About the Author

Peter Letourneau is the most widely published farm tractor author and editor in the world. He is a former Case dealer and has also worked for two international companies involved in agricultural equipment and chemicals. He is the author or editor of twenty-two books, all of which are still in print, including two other books on Case tractors and other titles on John Deere, International Harvester, Fordson, Oliver, Caterpillar, Minneapolis-Moline, and more. Presently, he makes his living as a full-time writer and publisher. He is married with four children, and makes his home in a Nineteenth-century Victorian home in Stillwater, Minnesota.

Index

Case Catalog with Crossmotor
The sun shone like a halo behind Case's Crossmotor tractor on this catalog cover.